AMERICAN ART & ARTISTS

Series Editor: BRENDA GILCHRIST

WINSLOW HOMER

WINSLOW HOMER

John Wilmerding

Praeger Publishers

New York · Washington · London

FRONTISPIECE:
Hurricane, Bahamas, 1898.
Watercolor, 14½ x 21 inches.
The Metropolitan Museum of Art. Amelia B. Lazarus Fund, 1910.

PRAEGER PUBLISHERS
111 Fourth Avenue, New York, N. Y. 10003, U.S.A.
5, Cromwell Place, London SW7 2JL, England

Published in the United States of America in 1972
by Praeger Publishers, Inc.

Library of Congress Catalog Card Number: 71-189930

Color illustrations printed in Great Britain

Printed in the United States of America

FOR JIM NACHTWEY AND DENIS O'NEILL,
good students and good friends

Contents

List of Illustrations

Black-and-White Illustrations

LIST OF ILLUSTRATIONS

BEFITTING ONE OF AMERICA's greatest painters, books on Winslow Homer have been published regularly since his lifetime. Not unexpectedly for a reclusive and original artist, criticism about him was uneven during his life, but shortly following his death in 1910, biographies were published that attempted to summarize the major aspects of his life and of his career. The writing on Homer has been in three principal phases: The first books just after his death were by William Howe Downes in 1911 and Kenyon Cox in 1914. These were largely reminiscences and appraisals made, respectively, by an art critic and a fellow painter who were Homer's contemporaries. The next major assessments came almost thirty years later with the pictorial survey by Forbes Watson of 1942 and Lloyd Goodrich's monograph of 1945, which has remained the definitive biography. The 1960's saw a new interpretation of Homer's career by Albert Gardner, who stressed the importance of the artist's 1866–67 trip to Paris. Philip Beam's biography of 1969 somewhat balances this approach with attention directed foremost to the later Maine years.

Within recent years, several major exhibitions of Homer's work have been mounted, and more modest books have dealt with special aspects of his career, such as his graphic art and his watercolors. The time now seems due for a fresh synthesis of these foregoing treatments in order to bring into new balance the unevenly accumulated information on different parts of Homer's life and career. Yet, the present study does not purport to uncover much new biographical material. Most of the facts of the artist's life are already available in the existing bibliography, and every Homer biographer has had to begin and end with the painter's cultivated reticence and guarded seclusion. Downes had attempted to solicit information firsthand from Homer, but his efforts were unsuccessful. The painter kindly but firmly wrote to Downes:

> It may seem ungrateful to you that after your twenty-five years of hard work in booming my pictures that I should not agree with you in regard to that proposed sketch of my life. But I think that it would probably kill me to have such a thing appear, and as the most interesting part of my life is of no concern to the public I must decline to give you any particulars in regard to it.*

In his own way, Homer is in effect telling us that we should scrutinize his art for the revelations of his life, the expressions of his innermost feelings and ideas. His forceful and memorable pictures ultimately become the "most interesting part" of his life. My major concerns here are to reexamine the paintings themselves, to consider afresh the development of his style and the meaning of his images, and to view Homer's work in the broader context of the arts in nineteenth-century America. I believe there is much to learn, for example, about his distinctive achievement in relating his Civil War sketches to the writing of Stephen Crane and Walt Whitman, his Gloucester watercolors to Mark Twain's stories, and his later seascapes in Maine to the mature works of Herman Melville. The special nature of Homer's essentially new realism at mid-century may profitably be viewed, as well, in the light of the photographic vision of Mathew Brady, Alexander Gardner, and Timothy O'Sullivan.

The occasional counterpoint of other artists may also illuminate certain aspects of Homer's career. Reference to Fitz Hugh Lane's early lithographic work will tell us much about Homer's own apprenticeship in the same graphic arts tradition, just as the genre painting of William Sidney Mount will set the stage for Homer's later genre style and subject matter. Homer's paintings in Gloucester deserve fuller comparison with the work of other artists painting there not long before or contemporary with him, namely Lane, William Morris Hunt, and Childe Hassam. There are also important comparisons to be explored between Homer and Eastman Johnson, Thomas Eakins, John Singer Sargent, and others. What follows, therefore, are considered speculations more than assertions of fact. But I hope that these various approaches and partial digressions will delineate a new understanding of Winslow Homer's artistic achievement.

For their considerate and thoughtful assistance, I should like to express my appreciation to Brenda Gilchrist, Ellyn Ann Childs, and Cherene Holland of Praeger Publishers; to Arthur Altschul; John Brooks of the Clark Art Institute, Williamstown, Mass.; Professor

* Quoted in Lloyd Goodrich, *Winslow Homer* (New York, 1945), p. 1.

Page 21
COLOR PLATE 1.
Skating in Central Park, c. 1860. Pen, brush, and watercolor on paper, 16 7/16 x 24½ inches. The St. Louis Art Museum.
Eliza McMillan Fund. (Detail.)

Above
COLOR PLATE 2.
Defiance: Inviting à Shot Before Petersburg, Virginia, 1864. Oil on panel, 12 x 18 inches. The Detroit Institute of Arts.
Gift of Dexter M. Ferry, Jr.

Below
COLOR PLATE 3.
Pitching Horseshoes, 1865. Oil on canvas, 26¾ x 53¾ inches. Courtesy, Fogg Art Museum, Harvard University. Gift of Mr. and Mrs. Frederick H. Curtiss.

Page 24
COLOR PLATE 4.
Prisoners from the Front, 1866. Oil on canvas, 24 x 38 inches. The Metropolitan Museum of Art. Gift of Mrs. Frank B. Porter, 1922.

painting, were a number of years younger. Among those Homer's exact age were Homer Dodge Martin, a poetic landscapist, and Elihu Vedder, a romantic and mystic who spent much of his time in Italy. Yet Homer's realism was very much of its time. The love of physicality, so evident in his rough landscapes and sturdy individuals, was as natural an expression of Victorian materialism as were the palpable objects in Harnett's still lifes, the rich textures in Sargent's portraits, or the weight of presence of Eakins's figures. Homer's singular independence and self-reliance, his practicality and care, along with his celebration of youth, endurance, and the out-of-doors, all seem to be distinctively American traits. Homer's art represents the culmination of that nineteenth-century reverence for the physical and moral force of nature.

Homer's first real awareness of nature came during his youth, in Boston's then-rural suburb of Cambridge. He was born in the family house at 25 Friend Street in Boston. The family soon moved to 7 Bulfinch Street near Bowdoin Square, and, when Winslow was about six, to Cambridge. They moved into a house on Massachusetts Avenue (then Main Street) and later into a larger dwelling on Garden Street that looked on to the Common. Of this period, G. W. Sheldon, a contemporary historian, wrote in 1878:

> [Homer] has a great liking for country life—a liking which he thinks had its origin in the meadows, ponds, fishing, and beautiful surroundings of that suburban place. To this day there is no recreation that Mr. Homer prefers to an excursion into the country.[2]

During childhood, Homer also developed what was to be a lifelong closeness to his older brother by two years, Charles Savage, Jr. A second brother, Arthur Benson, was five years younger than Winslow, and his greater separation in age and in distance (he later lived in Texas) never made possible the same intimacy as existed between the other two. In fact, Charlie's devoted assistance and support recalls the sympathetic help rendered by Theo van Gogh to his brother Vincent. The Homer boys played in the surrounding lanes and fields of Cambridge, and one suspects that warm recollections of his youth were an important ingredient in his later Gloucester watercolors of carefree children and summer pleasures. Winslow enrolled in the local Washington Grammar School, presumably to follow in his older brother's footsteps on to Harvard College. But circumstances intervened. As Charlie said: "When we moved to Cambridge the idea was to give us boys an education but I was the only one that wiggled through Harvard College. Win wanted to draw."[3] More of a factor was his father's financial losses in an ill-fated venture to California, lured by the gold rush of 1849.

The situation inspired one of Homer's earliest surviving drawings (ILL. 1–1). It was a combination of artistic borrowing, factual observation, and sheer imagination. Depicting his father aboard a rocket ship crossing the country above waving figures and playful weather vanes on the right, the drawing also shows the rocket, after crossing the mountains, falling amid a group of scurrying miners. Although occasioned by his father's departure, the imagery had a more immediate source in a popular lithograph published that year by Nathaniel Currier entitled *The Way They Go to California* (ILL. 1–2). In it, potential excavators are enthusiastically departing by rocket as well as by sailing vessel and dirigible for the West Coast. But Currier had derived his own composition from an English engraving of 1845 that showed *The Flight of Intellect: Mr. Golightly on a Steam Riding Rocket*.[4] Homer's adaptation is free and fanciful. He replaces the elaborately mechanical rocket of his sources with a sleek flying form resembling something between a bird and a fishing lure. His composition, while an improvised sketch, is more panoramic than the tightly closed and balanced design by Currier and thus more intuitively suited to the imagined conceptions of space flight. In a curious way, too, the flying rocket and mountain landscape are surprising antecedents of Homer's later Adirondack paintings, with their leaping fish and silhouetted hillsides against the sky (ILLS. 3–42 and 5–8).

His parents encouraged his interests—Homer's mother must have been delighted, and his father on one occasion sent him from London a set of lithographs on animal and human anatomy from which he might make copies. Their hopes for seeing Winslow go on to college thwarted, discussion focused about the time he was nineteen on his entering some business profession. When his father caught the notice in the paper placed by his friend John H. Bufford advertising for an apprentice lithographer, he saw it as just the opportunity for his son. "Boy wanted; apply to Bufford, lithographer; must have a taste for drawing; no other wanted,"[5] read the advertisement; the young Homer's inclinations seemed to suit the call exactly. Along with Thomas Moore, L. H. Bradford, and J. C. Sharp, Bufford was one of the foremost lithographic publishers of the day. All were successors to the large business established in Boston by William Pendleton in the 1830's. Bufford had earlier worked in New York, coming to work for Thayer in Boston in 1840. By the late 1840's, he had bought Thayer out and was issuing lithographs under his own imprint. When Homer came to work for him, probably in late 1854, Bufford was the leading figure in the business.[6] His firm was certainly one of the largest, employing about a hundred people and producing a large variety of prints. Typically, these included trade cards, advertising posters, magazine illustrations, town views, and music-sheet covers. It was in this last category that Homer began his productions for Bufford.

G. W. Sheldon claimed that Homer's first music-sheet illustrations were *O Whistle and I'll Come to You* and *Katy Darling*.[7] During the course of his two years' apprenticeship with Bufford, he worked on at least eight other music-sheet covers, which markedly increased in sophistication and originality as he proceeded. His earliest efforts were almost entirely derivative. His job usually consisted of the then commonplace practice of copying popular English prints. Other sources included prints already published by Bufford and by other firms, as well as photographs and specimen books.[8] All this was normal in the process of learning lithographic skills. For example, *O Whistle* most likely had an English source and *Katy Darling* was a variant on another Bufford illustration of 1851.

A MAN WITH LARGE IDEAS

As Homer gained in confidence and ability, he began to take more liberties with his drawing, making alterations of his sources. The lithographs during the second year of his apprenticeship show an increasing adaptability and competence. Typical were *The Wreath* (ILL. 1–9), which showed an oval portrait of Andrew Johnson, and *The Queen's Waltzes* (ILL. 1–3), a portrait of the young Queen Victoria in coronation robes. In the latter case, Homer based his drawing on an 1838 engraving by Samuel Cousins (ILL. 1–4) after the original painting by Alfred Chalon, but he reduced Chalon's full-length figure to a bust-length composition. Both portraits reveal Homer's rapidly acquired technical assurance: His drawing is clear and sharp, the textures varied. His figures are palpable, and the sense of space and light convincing.

By 1857, Homer was introducing new elements of his own, often humorous, into his illustrations. In one music sheet of 1855, *The Ratcatcher's Daughter* (ILL. 1–5), he had already enlivened the English source with an animated design of donkeys and other animals around the oval bordering the central figure. In two other music sheets, *Minnie Clyde* of 1857 and *Rogers' Quick Step* of 1856 (ILLS. 1–11 and 1–13), he added comic details of his own invention. In the former, he balances the cat on one side of Minnie Clyde's feet with a small toad on the other, whose long thin tongue is sticking out at the artist's initials; in the latter, Homer seems to parody the then current vogue of military songs and prints with his obviously mechanical repetition of toy soldiers in formation. Homer here demonstrates a combination of sure familiarity with various English prototypes and personal inventiveness in his handling of the medium.

Lithography had been invented in Germany at the end of the eighteenth century and introduced into the United States during the first quarter of the nineteenth century. It differed from earlier printmaking methods, notably woodcuts and engravings, which were essentially relief processes, in being planographic. That is, the image was drawn with a greasy crayon on the surface of a polished stone (rather than cut with a tool into a wood block or metal plate), and when moisture was applied to the stone, it adhered to those areas not touched by the crayon. Then the grease-based ink in turn clung to the drawing, being repelled by water-covered portions, and the drawing could be transferred to paper with a minimum of pressure. Altogether, it was an easier and cheaper graphic art form than earlier methods. It also permitted greater freedom of drawing, as well as softer and more varied textural effects, and Homer took advantage of these properties from the start of his career. Like all graphic arts, lithography relies foremost on the dual sensibilities for drawing and for tonal contrasts. Homer's only formal training, then, taught him to see and render form fundamentally in terms of line or silhouette and in terms of light and dark patterns. This was a mode of perception that he would retain and cultivate in all of his art throughout the rest of his career.

The borrowing from English sources for much of his work and that of his contemporaries at this time is not surprising. John Brandard was an especially inventive and popular

English artist, and with no copyright laws then in effect he was widely copied by American printmakers.[9] Boston tastes had long shown an affinity for English manners and styles. John Singleton Copley had left to spend the latter part of his career in London. Charles Bulfinch brought back to his buildings and plans for Boston the Adamesque style and English urban designs. W. H. Bartlett had published his *American Scenery* in London, and Robert Havell engraved John James Audubon's *Birds of America* there. In Boston specifically and in America generally, British books and illustrations had a natural appeal. By mid-century the ideas of John Ruskin were to receive wide circulation in the United States and have a pervasive influence on American artistic ideas.[10] For Homer, this early exposure to English art and ideas was to culminate in the 1880's with his second trip abroad, where his two years near Tynemouth would prove to be a fundamental turning point in his career.

Because of Homer's noted reticence, controversy has focused on just how much his art was affected at various stages in his life by outside, and particularly European, influences. With only the works themselves to go on, historians will probably continue to argue this issue. It does seem clear that his early training at Bufford's introduced him to a strong tradition of English illustration. But it is also likely that his two years of work in Boston further made him aware of native accomplishments in the arts. After all, he arrived at Bufford's at the high point of prosperity for such lithographic firms. Their preeminence was in large measure due to an earlier generation of Boston artists—Robert Cooke, David Claypoole Johnson, and Fitz Hugh Lane—who had themselves begun as lithographers and brought the technique to fruition during the 1830's and 40's. The delight in anecdote and comic detail that we note in Homer's music sheets was already well established in the work of his Boston predecessors. In fact, a comparison of his illustrations with theirs suggests that Homer consciously continued both their style and iconography.

Much of Homer's sense of caricature and playful humor would seem to derive from D. C. Johnson's cartoons and satiric drawings. Homer's interest in facial expression, his rendering of jauntily waving children in *The Wheelbarrow Polka* (1856), the attention to the tattered clothing of the comical figure in *The Ratcatcher's Daughter* (1855), all appear to owe a debt to Johnson, whose work should certainly have been familiar to anyone following in the same line of illustration. It is even conceivable that Homer may have known of other genre artists. For example, his youthful and gesturing figures also share affinities with the contemporary paintings of George Caleb Bingham and William Sidney Mount. Engravings after Bingham's *Jolly Flatboatmen* and *Raftsmen Playing Cards* and Mount's *Bargaining for a Horse* and *Farmers Nooning* were receiving wide circulation through the American Art-Union and other institutions at this time. One of Homer's few sketches to survive from this period is an 1855 drawing of boys setting a squirrel trap (ILL. 1–6), which is especially reminiscent of Mount's painting *The Dead Fall* (ILL. 1–7). Another picture of Mount's, *Catching Rabbits* (Suffolk Museum, Stony Brook, N.Y.), was also engraved and may well have been an image familiar to the young Homer.

An equally probable influence on his music-sheet illustrations was Lane, who had himself executed some dozen music-sheet covers and numerous other lithographic prints between 1835 and 1845. A native of Gloucester, Lane also had begun his career training as an apprentice in William Pendleton's shop. Although most of his music sheets were completed before 1840, he continued to produce lithographed views even after turning to a full-time painting career around 1848. Lane was in Boston at work on several lithographs in the very years that Homer was working for Bufford, and at least one, *The Steam Demi-Bark "Antelope,"* was lithographed at Bufford's firm. Lane was by this time solidly established as an artist; in 1851, a Boston newspaper called him "our best marine painter." It is hard to imagine that a younger painter with such similar aspirations and inclinations would not have come to know Lane's oils and lithographs.

Lane had completed in 1841 a memorial print of *William H. Harrison, Late President of the United States* (ILL. 1–8), a possible source for Homer's sheet-music illustrations for *The Wreath*, 1856 (ILL. 1–9), dedicated "to His Excellency, Andrew Johnson, Gov. of Tenn.," and for *Katy Darling*, 1854 (ILL. 1–10), with its Byronic mourner contemplating his loved one's gravestone before a woodland vista. Both Lane's subjects and technique seem to have carried over into Homer's apprentice work. Lane was especially adept at rendering the oval vignette of the central illustration as well as the decorative details embroidering the border of the page. His marine interests are evident in both the principal subject and embellishing details of the *Song of the Fisher's Wife* (ILL. 1–12), but the moody girl, receding landscape view, crisp textural details, and variegated light effects all appear in *Minnie Clyde* (ILL. 1–11).

Several of Lane's militia music sheets could have served as the basis for Homer's drawing of *Rogers' Quick Step* (ILL. 1–13). This was a favorite type of illustration for Lane during his apprenticeship, and among those produced by him were *Capt. E. G. Austin's Quick Step,* which showed a formation of soldiers marching over a hill with Boston harbor in the background; *The Norfolk Guards Quick Step* (ILL. 1–14), depicting a soldier in ceremonial costume standing on a town green with several houses behind him; and *The Salem Mechanick Quick Step* (ILL. 1–15), illustrating the militia formation lined up on the Salem Common before their encampment and Samuel McIntire's commemorative arch. The woodenly repeated figures and tents behind are a striking antecedent of Homer's later treatment of the subject.

Also, in 1855, Lane was in Boston to work on two of his finest large color lithographs, of Gloucester and Castine, Maine, both published that year. Is it possible that accomplished prints such as these provided Homer with his first inclination of the subjects that a successful artist might approach on his own? Homer was required by the terms of his agreement with Bufford to remain until his twenty-first birthday, in February, 1857. But he was clearly chafing under the limitations on his personal and artistic freedom. Many years later the painter's friend, John W. Beatty, described Homer's large lithograph done in 1856 of the

Massachusetts Senate, an oval composition inset with individual portraits of the forty-two legislators. Although demonstrating Homer's technical capabilities, it was the source of some dissatisfaction for him. Beatty quoted him as saying, "The price received for each portrait by the proprietor [Bufford] was thirty-five dollars, while I meanwhile received five dollars per week."[11] Disgruntled and ready to work on his own, he left Bufford's when he came of age and "never again worked for wages." G. W. Sheldon added that "his sojourn there was a treadmill existence. Two years at that grindstone unfitted him for further bondage; and, since the day he left it, he has called no man his master."[12]

The path from apprentice lithographer to successful painter had already been set for him by artists like Johnson, Lane, and Benjamin Champney. Thus, in this critical and not always happy early period, Homer probably got his first taste of English and American art; both seemed to be currents that would appear more strongly defined in later aspects of his art. One cannot help but wonder if an early acquaintance with Lane's work might not have been a factor both in Homer's resolution to become an artist and in his decision to paint for several summers in Gloucester two decades later.

Not wishing to work further for anyone but himself, Homer determined to continue doing illustrations as a means of support. After leaving Bufford's, he moved into the Ballou Publishing House building on Winter Street, where he set up his studio and began to work in wood engraving. This method of printmaking involved drawing on a finely polished wooden block. Homer sometimes drew directly on the block and other times on tracing paper with the lines transferred through pressure to the surface beneath (see ILLS. 3–1 and 3–2). Then the block was cut away in the areas between lines, leaving the drawn lines raised in relief to be inked and printed. The medium did not permit the soft textures or free drawing of lithography, primarily because of the resistance between wood and cutting tool, but it did provide even stronger contrasts of tone and sharper lines for defining details or outlining forms. A French engraver by the name of Damoreau gave Homer some assistance in learning the rudiments of the technique. Damoreau worked at Ballou's and later engraved many of Homer's illustrations for *Ballou's Pictorial Drawing-Room Companion.* The magazine was a properly Bostonian publication, conservative in content and decorum, suitably but discreetly informative for the entire family.

Homer soon felt himself sufficiently confident in the new medium to submit his first illustration to *Ballou's,* a portrait of *Rembrandt Peale,* probably based on a photograph. It appeared in the issue of June 6, 1857, and a week later a more ambitious illustration of his was published on the front page. It showed a lively scene entitled *Corner of Winter, Washington and Summer-Streets, Boston* (ILL. 1–16) and was filled with men in top hats, fashionable ladies, playing children, street vendors, and horse-drawn carriages. Strictly reportorial, it nevertheless possessed an animation and immediacy that was new for *Ballou's.* The lead article for the issue began above by commenting:

The local view upon this page, drawn expressly for us by Mr. Winslow Homer, a promising young artist of this city, is exceedingly faithful in architectural detail and spirited in character, and represents one of the busiest and most brilliant spots in all Boston.[13]

In the months that followed, Homer undertook numerous assignments for the magazine, most of the illustrations being Boston views or scenes from daily life. One of the more comic was the *Husking Party Finding the Red Ears* (engraved for Homer by Damoreau), which appeared on November 28, 1857 (ILL. 1–17). There, a nighttime party of young ladies and gentlemen are husking corn and stealing kisses in a barn lit by lanterns. It is still a cluttered design, although adroit enough in the handling of artificial light. Before long Homer was saving his best drawings to send to the recently founded *Harper's Weekly* in New York. Through 1858 and 1859, he contributed to both *Ballou's* and *Harper's*; among those drawings sent to the latter was a new, more confidently executed version of *Husking the Corn in New England*, November 13, 1858 (ILL. 1–18), and scenes of football matches at Harvard. He continued to depict decorous figures crossing Boston's streets or Common, and later skating and enjoying themselves in Central Park, New York (COLOR PLATE 1). His training as an illustrator and his probable awareness of the American genre tradition naturally led his observant eye to scenes of leisure and fashion. His optimistic recording of American life was a characteristic reflection of the country's accumulating self-confidence. Faith in the virtues of national identity and celebration of everyday life had both political and intellectual expressions earlier in the century, such as Jacksonian Democracy, the Monroe Doctrine, and Manifest Destiny, or Emerson's essay on the American Scholar. These were embodiments of a newly felt collective force and geographical inviolability. There was self-satisfaction in the belief that the common man in a democracy could attain the White House. Equally fervent was the faith that American art, literature, and thought bore their own stamp. The national character strove at once for definition and for influence. Events like the opening of the Erie Canal and the admission of newly acquired territories as states to the Union further enhanced a sense of continental power. In the tradition of Mount and Bingham before him, Homer in his early work recorded with enthusiasm and sympathy the ordinary manners, pursuits, and pleasures of his fellow citizens. Both before and after the Civil War, his illustrations are, for the most part, images of well-being.

With the acceptance of Homer's first contributions in 1857, *Harper's* continued to print his illustrations regularly, and in the fall of 1859 Homer determined to move to New York to be at the center of artistic activities. *Ballou's* was about to return to a purely literary magazine without illustrations, but Homer had already been submitting his best work to *Harper's*. After his experience at Bufford's shop, he was unwilling to be employed full-time, and so began what was to be a long and productive association as free-lance artist. He continued to submit sketches of local town views, but now of New York's instead of Boston's streets and parks. Increasingly his drawing became more controlled, his rendering of light more subtle, his compositions more spacious and less cluttered. It is one of the few periods in his life in which he depicts people so physically active. Soon he would begin to isolate figures in smaller groups or alone and show them in more stable postures and compositions.

In New York, Homer evidently took some art lessons and visited the local art galleries. Sheldon tells us that he

> attended a drawing-school in Brooklyn [as well as] the night-school of the Academy of Design, then in Thirteenth Street, under Professor Cummings's tuition. . . . In 1861 he determined to paint. For a month, in the old Dodworth Building near Grace Church, he took lessons in painting of Rondel, an artist from Boston, who once a week, on Saturdays, taught him how to handle his brush, set his palette, etc.[14]

Frederic Rondel was a competent though rather sentimental landscape painter who seems to have had little artistic influence on the development of Homer's style beyond the technical instruction he provided in oils. Of equal if not greater importance for Homer, however, was his introduction to and association with other artists working in the city, including Eastman Johnson, whose painting in the next decade would have much in common with Homer's. In 1861, Homer moved into the New York University building on Washington Square, where both he and Johnson maintained studios through the 1860's and early 70's.[15] As Thomas Bailey Aldrich described them, these quarters sounded somewhat inhibiting, if functional:

> We shall never be able to understand why eight or ten of these pleasant fellows have located themselves in the New York University. There isn't a more gloomy structure outside of one of Mrs. Radcliffe's romances; and we hold that few men could pass a week in those lugubrious chambers without adding a morbid streak to their natures,—the present genial inmates to the contrary notwithstanding. . . .
>
> It has taken us some time to reach Mr. Homer's *atelier*, for it is on the third or fourth floor. But the half-finished picture on his easel, the two or three crayon sketches on the walls, (military subjects), and the splendid view from his window, cause us to forget that last long flight of stairs.
>
> The studio itself does not demand particular notice. It is remarkable for nothing but its contracted dimensions: it seems altogether too small for a man to have a large idea in.[16]

Shortly after Homer had moved into the university studios, Lincoln came through town en route to his inauguration. Homer made a sketch of him speaking from the balcony of the Astor House, and for *Harper's* he also drew the inauguration in Washington. Soon after the Civil War began, the magazine commissioned Homer to illustrate life at the front.

His drawings continued to appear regularly in the pages of *Harper's*, but the war years brought important changes to his artistic life. He now began to paint pictures in oil; his style in both this medium and his engraved illustrations revealed a decisive new maturity.

1-1. *Man on a Rocket*, 1849. Pencil on paper, 3¾ x 15⅛ inches. Courtesy, Museum of Fine Arts, Boston. Gift of Edwin Klyeth.

1-2. Nathaniel Currier: *The Way They Go to California*, 1849. Lithograph, 10¼ x 17⅝ inches. The Old Print Shop, New York.

Left
1-3. *The Queen's Waltzes*, 1856. Lithographed music-sheet cover, 13¼ x 10 inches. Library of Congress.

Right
1-4. Samuel Cousins after Alfred Chalon: *Queen Victoria in Coronation Robes*, 1838. Mezzotint, 30½ x 20¾ inches. The Trustees of The British Museum, London.

35

1-5. *The Ratcatcher's Daughter*, 1855. Lithographed music-sheet cover, 13¼ x 10 inches. The Metropolitan Museum of Art. Harris Brisbane Dick Fund, 1936.

1-6. *Setting a Squirrel Trap*, 1855. Pencil and watercolor on paper, 8⅜ x 11½ inches. Cooper-Hewitt Museum of Decorative Arts and Design, Smithsonian Institution, New York.

1-7. William Sidney Mount: *The Dead Fall* or *Trap Sprung*, 1844. Oil on panel, 12¾ x 17 inches. Suffolk Museum and Carriage House, Melville Collection, Stony Brook, Long Island, New York.

Above left

1-8. Fitz Hugh Lane: *William H. Harrison, Late President of the United States*, 1841. Lithographed commemorative print, 12 x 9 inches. Library of Congress.

Above center

1-9. *The Wreath*, 1856. Lithographed music-sheet cover, 13¼ x 10 inches. Courtesy, Museum of Fine Arts, Boston.

Above right

1-10. *Katy Darling*, 1854. Lithographed music-sheet cover, 13¼ x 10 inches. Courtesy, Museum of Fine Arts, Boston.

Below

1-11. *Minnie Clyde*, 1857. Lithographed music-sheet cover, 13⅛ x 9⅝ inches. Library of Congress.

Left

1-12. Fitz Hugh Lane: *Song of the Fisher's Wife*, 1840. Lithographed music-sheet cover, 12 x 9 inches. Library of Congress.

Right

1-13. *Rogers' Quick Step*, 1856. Lithographed music-sheet cover, 13 x 10 inches. The Bostonian Society, Boston.

Left

1-14. Fitz Hugh Lane: *The Norfolk Guards Quick Step*, 1840. Lithographed music-sheet cover, 13½ x 8¾ inches. Private collection.

Right

1-15. Fitz Hugh Lane: *The Salem Mechanick Light Infantry Quick Step*, 1836. Lithographed music-sheet cover, 12½ x 9½ inches. Private collection.

1-16. *Corner of Winter, Washington and Summer Streets, Boston*, 1857. Wood engraving, 7 x 9½ inches. Courtesy, Trustees of Dartmouth College, Hanover, New Hampshire.

Above
1-17. *Husking Party Finding the Red Ears*, 1857. Wood engraving, 6⅜ x 9⅜ inches. Courtesy, Trustees of Dartmouth College, Hanover, New Hampshire.

Below
1-18. *Husking the Corn in New England*, 1858. Wood engraving, 10 x 13½ inches. Courtesy, Trustees of Dartmouth College, Hanover, New Hampshire.

2

Painting What Is Seen and Known

THE OPENING SUMMER of the Civil War, Homer returned to Massachusetts to stay with his parents, recently moved to Belmont. His early images related to the conflict were not of military action but of young ladies writing letters or sewing clothes for the soldiers. During the fall of 1861, he made an initial trip to the front. The Union Army at that time was relatively inactive, recovering as it was from its losses at Bull Run and reorganizing its ranks under General George B. McClellan. Homer's first illustration of war life, *A Bivouac Fire on the Potomac* (ILL. 2-2), appeared in *Harper's* on December 21, 1861. Reminiscent of his earlier cornhusking scenes, it depicts a large group of figures arranged around the artificial light of a campfire.

During the spring of 1862, he returned to join the Army of the Potomac for part of the Peninsular campaign. After watching the troops depart from Washington on April 1, he remained with them through the siege of Yorktown. During this period, he made a number of pen and pencil sketches of soldiers grouped around their camps near Yorktown (Addison Gallery, Andover; and Boston Museum of Fine Arts). These provided the basis for oils later undertaken when he returned to New York, such as *In Front of Yorktown* (Yale University Art Gallery, New Haven). During the summer of 1862, Sheldon recounts that "he bought a tin box containing brushes, colors, oils, and various equipment and started out into the country to paint from Nature."[1] Drawing on his limited experience with Rondel and now committed to working directly out-of-doors, Homer began to work on his first significant oil paintings.

An early oil served as the basis for one of his most forceful Civil War illustrations in *Harper's*. He worked on the painting in his New York studio after returning from the front and subsequently drew the image on wood for the engraving that appeared on

41

November 15, 1862, entitled *The Army of the Potomac—A Sharp-shooter on Picket Duty* (ILL. 2–1). Unlike much of his graphic work to date, the picture concentrated on a single figure seen close-up, in this instance, a Union soldier seated in the branches of a tree taking aim on some enemy out of view. Compared with his early music sheets (ILLS. 1–10 and 1–11), this shows an economy of design and detail. Using a striking vantage point above ground, Homer contrasts the strong verticals, horizontals, and diagonals of the tree's trunk and branches with the soldier's legs, torso, and rifle. He reserves the sharpest details and silhouetting for the centrally placed figure of the soldier. The sense of dramatic immediacy is successfully achieved, both by the close point of view and by the implication of impending action outside the composition, devices he would return to many years later in his painting *The Life Line* (COLOR PLATE 29).

From the same trip also resulted two of his rare action scenes, *A Cavalry Charge* (ILL. 2–3) and *A Bayonet Charge*, both published in July issues of *Harper's*. But it was the *Sharp-shooter* rather than these crowded compositions that set the direction for the style and format of his major war canvases to follow. For example, two oils done the next year, *Punishment for Intoxication* (Canajoharie Art Gallery, New York) and *Home Sweet Home* (Collection of Mr. and Mrs. Nathan Shaye) show only two soldiers against the receding camp background; while another engraving for *Harper's* in 1863, *The Approach of the British Pirate "Alabama"* (ILL. 2–4), depicts five figures on a boat's deck clearly silhouetted against the plain expanse of sea and sky behind. Homer was now composing with a surer sense of major dark and light patterns and of the compositional relationship between figural forms and the framing edges of the page. This may have been partially due to an increasing astuteness of observation, his accumulated experience as an illustrator, and the immediacy of action itself seen firsthand.

Another likely source of Homer's more simplified style and stabilized designs was contemporary photography. Although some photographs had been taken of soldiers in the Mexican War, they were essentially posed portraits, and only during the Crimean War in the mid-1850's did the camera become an influential means of documentation, with views readily publishable in magazines and journals back home soon after the actual events. By the time of the U.S. Civil War, Mathew Brady, already solidly established as a highly popular portrait daguerreotypist and photographer in New York, was prepared with his assistants, Alexander Gardner and Timothy O'Sullivan, to take their camera equipment to the field for direct photographing of the conflict. Where Homer had the stimulus of publishing his drawings in *Harper's*, Brady and his colleagues had the backing of government leaders to get close to the scenes of war.[2] Artists like Homer, Albert Bierstadt, Alfred R. Waud, Conrad Wise Chapman, and others were not the only correspondents in the field depicting the war's events; the photographer's traveling buggy became an equally familiar sight on the battlefields and in the camps.

Many of Homer's sketches and some of his engravings of this period have an anecdotal or literary quality that ties them to the traditions of magazine illustration in which he was trained. Yet, his new emphasis at this time on pictorial design and the purely visual character of some scenes suggests a familiarity with the images recorded by his colleagues with cameras. The strong two-dimensional organization of forms, the awareness of the framing edge, the sense of stasis and pose were all typical of the photographer's eye, and to one degree or another these aspects now appear in Homer's work. The striking emphasis on silhouetted forms—whether people or architectural ruins—is characteristic of many photographs by Brady and George Barnard, notably those taken by the former of the ruins at Richmond, Virginia, and those by the latter of Chattanooga, Tennessee; Charleston, South Carolina; and Atlanta, Georgia (ILL. 2–6). In the same years that these were being published, Homer was employing similar devices in the composition of his paintings; for example, his *Defiance: Inviting a Shot Before Petersburg, Virginia* of 1864 (COLOR PLATE 2) shows a lone soldier starkly isolated against the horizon line and the broad sweep of sky.

Only a few years later, in Paris for several months during 1867, Homer based at least one picture on a French photograph (ILLS. 2–31 and 2–33), and the style of his Civil War work would indicate an even earlier awareness of photography. In particular, his use of the close-up point of view, the occasionally cropped or carefully framed compositions, the emphasis on visual form rather than anecdotal content would appear to derive from images caught by Brady and his assistants. Compare the *Sharp-shooter* or the drawings of men on the battlefield (ILLS. 2–5 and 2–8) to photographs of dead soldiers taken by Gardner, O'Sullivan, or Brady (ILL. 2–7). Brady consciously exploits the expressiveness of his close vantage and the framing planes of ground and ditch to isolate the stark meaning of human mortality. In a similar way Homer has stressed the immediacy of his subject by bringing the viewer in close to the subject and by setting off the figure or group with a simple but powerful monumentality.

Two of Homer's most important paintings from the Civil War possess this sense of posed stability so characteristic of photography: *Pitching Horseshoes* of 1865 and *Prisoners from the Front* of 1866 (COLOR PLATES 3 and 4). Like the photographers, Homer seldom illustrated or painted scenes of action. There is no evidence that he shied away from them. The fact that the photographer necessarily had to record the unmoving—neither the camera equipment nor developing techniques yet permitted anything approaching stop-action views—naturally drew him to the dead on battlefields after the action, soldiers relaxing in camp, group formations or portraits, and architectural ruins. As one contemporary paper wrote, "The photographer who follows in the wake of modern armies must be content with conditions of repose and with the still life which remains when the fighting is over."[3] Through such subjects, photographers captured the profound humanity and inhumanity of war, and Homer's first really serious works have a similar dignity and objectivity.

PAINTING WHAT IS SEEN AND KNOWN

The rather static quality and posed sobriety of both *Pitching Horseshoes* and *Prisoners from the Front* are reminiscent of the many photographs by Brady and O'Sullivan of soldiers posed casually or formally in groups (ILL. 2–9). In both cases, the generally large figures are disposed laterally across the canvas, seen clearly silhouetted against the background. As he would do so often in later pictures, Homer here relates the groups of figures in subtle internal balances: In the one it is the participants juxtaposed with the spectators, and in the other it is a single well-groomed Union officer seen in profile contrasted with the tattered group of Confederate prisoners and their guards repeated frontally. The strong, simple design and the unpretentious realism are notably close to Gustave Courbet's *Interment at Ornans* (Musée du Louvre, Paris) and *Bonjour Monsieur Courbet* (ILL. 2–10), painted about a decade earlier, illustrating the common currents running through mid-nineteenth-century painting in France and America. But Homer's strength of design and brushwork, his vigorous coloring, and the feeling of directness in recording the ordinary lend to his work a special force. Along with the photographers, he was creating a new type of realism in nineteenth-century art, which would mature and deepen during the remainder of his career.

A new realism also appears in American literature at this time. The Civil War itself was a stark reality that signaled the end of many romantic fantasies held by Americans in the first half of the century. Grand visions now yielded to immediate and practical problems. Art and literature reflected this shift in style and attitude.[4] Walt Whitman, for example, was creating a new poetic language, whose informality and directness shares much in common with Homer's straightforward images. In 1855, Whitman issued the first edition of his *Leaves of Grass*, revising and adding to it over the next few years, and during the Civil War he volunteered to work as an army nurse in Washington hospitals, an experience that he vividly described later in *Specimen Days*. His sense of the suffering from the war was perhaps more intimate than Homer's, but their firsthand experiences contributed to an essentially new direction in American art and literature. In writing about the war, Whitman not only spoke with a fresh poetic voice but also called for a new language with energetic rhythm and form that would suit his subject. *Eighteen Sixty-One* begins:

> Arm'd year—year of struggle,
> No dainty rhymes or sentimental love verses for
>   you terrible year,
> Not you as some pale poetling seated at a desk
>   lisping cadenzas piano,
> But as a strong man erect, clothed in blue clothes,
>   advancing, carrying a rifle on your shoulder,
> With well-gristled body and sunburnt face and hands,
>   with a knife in your belt at your side,
> As I heard you shouting loud, your sonorous voice
>   ringing across the continent . . .[5]

In their respective art forms, Whitman and Homer turn away from the patently rhetorical and philosophical character of earlier painting and writing. Without bombast, but with enthusiasm and sympathy, both men described the ordinary aspects and commonly shared experiences of American life. The broad philosophical generalizations of Emerson, James Fenimore Cooper, and Thomas Cole yielded to the specific, the concrete, and the mundane with Whitman and Homer. Their robust celebration of the here-and-now ultimately came to define and express a distinctively American vision of national promise.

Fiction in the second half of the century underwent parallel changes. When Stephen Crane wrote *The Red Badge of Courage* in 1893, he inherited and transformed the idiom of vernacular realism that first appeared in response to the Civil War. Writing equally about inner and outer conflicts, Crane relied on the personal point of view and accuracy of vision for his effect. The opening lines of *The Red Badge of Courage* are characteristic of his precise descriptions and reliance on factuality: "The cold passed reluctantly from the earth, and the retiring fogs revealed an army stretched out on the hills, resting."[6] The narrative is told from the point of view of one very ordinary young soldier; his naïveté and fear are apparent as we follow the events of clashing armies around him. Crane stresses the anonymity of war by usually referring to the central character (who is by no means a hero) as "the youth." He refers to wounds as laconically and matter-of-factly as Eakins painted blood on the hands of Dr. Gross or as O'Sullivan photographed "the harvest of death" at Gettysburg. The sense of being within the action, not above or outside it, and the confrontation of the realities of war face-to-face, unembellished and unromanticized, created an expression of particular force: "Under foot there were a few ghastly forms motionless. They lay twisted in fantastic contortions. Arms were bent and heads were turned in incredible ways."[7]

The view of men at war seen by the youth is close to both Brady and Homer: "The battle was like the grinding of an immense and terrible machine to him. Its complexities and powers, its grim processes, fascinated him. He must go close and see it produce corpses" (ILLS. 2–3 and 2–7).[8] At another point Crane writes, "And the most startling thing was to learn suddenly that he was very insignificant."[9] It was this overwhelming feeling of anonymity and insignificance in the face of larger, unmeasurable forces that the war artists and writers saw as a common experience. Their emphasis on individuals revealed on one level their wish to record the surface details of war life accurately, and on another their profound sense of man's humanity and mortality.

Occasionally, Homer painted a more distant view of the combat. His *Skirmish in the Wilderness* (ILL. 2–11) of 1864 is rather like Albert Bierstadt's *Attack on a Union Picket Post* (ILL. 2–12), painted two years before: Both show an anonymous group of soldiers shooting through a clearing in the woods, whose location is unknown, at the unseen enemy. Homer also did an engraving similar in subject for *Harper's* in 1862, *The Army of the Potomac—Our Outlying Picket in the Woods* (ILL. 2–13). Crane describes similar scenes:

The brigade was halted in the fringe of a grove. The men crouched among the trees and pointed their restless guns out at the fields. They tried to look beyond the smoke.... The men took positions behind a curving line of rifle pits that had been turned up, like a large furrow, along the line of woods. Before them was a level stretch, peopled with short, deformed stumps. From the woods beyond came the dull popping of the skirmishers and pickets, firing in the fog.[10]

Another artist who painted a number of Civil War subjects, very possibly under Homer's influence, was Eastman Johnson. The two men returned to work in nearby studios in the New York University building throughout this time, and it would be logical for them to have exchanged ideas on subjects of mutual interest. Born in 1824, Johnson was a native of Maine and in the early 1840's at work in a Boston lithography shop, most likely Bufford's.[11] Thus, the two men would have had much in common to discuss. Johnson had gone to Düsseldorf for study during the early 1850's and preceded Homer by a year or two in taking up quarters in the university building. With the outbreak of war, he too went to the front and over the next few years found himself present at several major battles, among them the first Bull Run, Antietam, Manassas, and Gettysburg.[12] While he did make some drawings and oil studies at the time, he did not complete the final oils until a few years after the war was over. Biographers of Homer and Johnson have so far uncovered no concrete evidence of the two artists' having been directly affected by each other, preferring instead to see their artistic developments as parallel and mutually complementary at most.[13] But both artists were members of the National Academy of Design (Johnson was elected in 1859, Homer in 1864), and from the 1860's on each had pictures exhibited fairly regularly at the annual exhibitions. Alike in background and training, in choice of subjects and stylistic development, exhibiting and working side by side, the two could not have been unaware of each other's art. To the contrary, many of their paintings of the 1860's and 70's suggest, not necessarily close collaboration, but certainly an evolutionary exchange of influences.

One of Homer's lithographs in his series called *Campaign Sketches*, done in 1863, was *The Letter from Home*, a subject that Johnson painted in oil four years later (ILLS. 2–16 and 2–17). The media and the setting are different, but similar are the generally diagonally arranged compositions, the contrasting light and dark forms of soldier and nurse, and the placement of a table and mailbag, and so on, at the lower right. Equally close are Homer's drawings of cavalry soldiers on horseback done in 1863–64 (Boston Museum of Fine Arts and ILL. 2–15) and Johnson's *Wounded Drummer Boy* (ILL. 2–14), based on an incident seen at Antietam in 1862. Johnson did a preparatory drawing about 1864, an oil study a couple of years after that, and the finished picture in 1871. The images by both artists have a sense of spontaneity and movement quite unlike William Morris Hunt's *Drummer Boy* (Collection Samuel H. Wolcott, Boston) of about 1861, which shows a young lad beating a drum in the call to arms. But whereas Hunt's figure stands solidly on a pedestal and is portrayed with a strong frontality and verticality, Homer's officer and Johnson's drummer are in excited motion, composed in forceful diagonals. They further share an emphasis on expressive silhouetting and on sharply alternating patterns of light and dark across the figures' clothing. Although Johnson's work is clearly more anecdotal than Homer's (the National Academy catalogue for 1872 carried several sentences of description for *The Wounded Drummer Boy*), it was nonetheless based on actual observation and included a portrait of the artist's nephew. As such, both its style and approach to recording fact are strikingly similar to Homer's at this point. Further evidence of a stylistic relationship between the two painters' work occurs again in the next decade.

For Homer, meanwhile, his pictures met early with favorable attention. He submitted his Civil War scenes to the National Academy in 1863 and 1864, when he was elected first to associate and then full membership. Thanks to some help from his brother Charles, he sold his first paintings, and the encouragement was sufficient to prod him on. *Prisoners from the Front* was a major success: It brought high critical praise and was soon acquired by a prominent New York collector. At the same time, he had attained personal confidence and artistic maturity. With the war over, he was free to paint full time if he wished and to paint what he wished. Another period of learning and accomplishment was over. Another was beginning.

Although Homer maintained his studio in New York during the Civil War, and resided in the city through the 1870's, he was not interested in painting the urban scene or life. Almost immediately, he set out for the countryside, seeking subject matter in rural Pennsylvania, upstate New York, the White Mountains of New Hampshire, and the coastal resorts of New Jersey. He turned from the masculine world of conflict to the feminine one of leisure and relaxation. Typical was his illustration for *Frank Leslie's Illustrated Newspaper* on January 13, 1866, *Our National Winter Exercise—Skating*, depicting groups of young men and ladies taking turns and spills on the ice. Almost all his graphic work now reflected his new economy of design and strong contrasts of light and dark patterns. Reminders of the war occasionally cropped up: One illustration shows an injured veteran on a carriage ride with a young lady. Homer does not recall the bitterness and horror of the war; rather he chooses one of the many scenes of men and women back together again.

In one poignant but unsentimental picture, he did seem to summarize his feelings about the war. His *Veteran in a New Field* (ILL. 2–22) of 1865 is a perfect image of survival and of the cessation of hostilities. A solitary figure expends his energies and exercises his discipline on cutting down the hay instead of enemies. His turned back establishes an anonymous and universal quality that enhances this reunion of man and nature, this juxtaposition of age and newness. The strongly defined vertical figure against the plain horizontal bands of hay and sky well suits the sense of quiet endurance. The subject had already attracted Homer the year before when he painted *Haymaking* (ILL. 2–25), a less serious and more anecdotal picture. Together they suggest that he may have had in mind William Sidney Mount's *Farmer Whetting His Scythe* of 1848 (ILL. 2–23). As mentioned earlier, Homer might

PAINTING WHAT IS SEEN AND KNOWN

already have known Mount's paintings and engravings of youths catching rabbits when he made his own drawing in 1855 of boys setting a squirrel trap (ILLS. 1–6 and 1–7). Certain compositional devices used by Homer in several paintings of the 1860's and 70's certainly recall Mount, as do the subjects of youthful pastimes (see ILLS. 3–18 to 3–20 and COLOR PLATE 13). Homer returned to another variation on the theme in his small engraving of *Green Apples* (ILL. 2–24) for *Our Young Folks* in 1868.

During 1865 and 1866, Homer painted pictures of young ladies going about everyday chores, such as *The Morning Bell*, 1866 (COLOR PLATE 8), or pursuing fashionable pleasures, as in the several croquet scenes dating from this time (COLOR PLATE 5 and ILL. 2–18). The latter make remarkable comparisons with Monet's paintings of similar subjects also dating from the same years (ILL. 2–19). Homer began his series before he left for Paris in late 1866, so the similarities that exist between the artists at this point are probably more a matter of parallel stylisic development than of any exchange of influences. In fact, the differences are more noteworthy and revealing. Already Monet's painting is characteristic of early French Impressionism in its effort to record forms as seen under bright outdoor light. By means of broken patches of pure color and heightened intensities, the French artists sought to re-create those colors as they struck the retina of the eye. Essentially, their interest was formal; that is, they were concerned more with how the eye perceived objects than with the objects themselves. The opposite was the case with Homer.

In Monet's *Women in a Garden* the entire tonality of the picture is lighter than in Homer's work. The dresses of the women and the foliage of the trees are treated as variably sized patches of color, which exist more in their own right than as a means of modeling the solid forms beneath. The space of the picture is relatively shallow: The figures and the garden path tend to press forward to the picture plane. Monet increasingly brought everything up to the picture surface and in late Impressionism permitted all his forms to be dissolved into accents of light and color. Homer, by contrast, retains the palpability of his figures and the space in which they are placed. Color is more localized and descriptive, aiding in the process of modeling the rounded forms of the hats, arms, and hoop skirts. The space of the croquet lawn strongly recedes toward the horizon as a firm platform under the figures.[14] The deep thrust into depth and the solidity of forms, so uncharacteristic of Impressionism, were perceptions retained by Homer even after his Paris trip, as is evident in *Long Branch, New Jersey* (COLOR PLATE 12) of 1869.

Still, the precise chronology of these works in Homer's career is not yet clear, nor just what relationship they bear to the contemporary paintings by Monet and Boudin (ILL. 4–3). But even if Homer could have seen the French examples, it is important to understand the essentially American character of his art that he retained. This was equally true of Eastman Johnson's style at this time. Again possibly sharing ideas with Homer, Johnson was soon to take up similar subjects, as his *Hollyhocks* of 1876 (ILL. 2–21) indicates. This, too, is a subject close in style and feeling to Monet, but as in Homer it is conceived with a much fuller range of dark to light tonalities, rather than the intentionally restricted French palette of high intensities. Nor does Johnson permit that tendency toward the dissolution of form by means of pure color touches that occurs in Monet; both figures and space retain their three-dimensional reality. Note how Johnson's garden path firmly leads the eye from the foreground plane deep into the background, where two women stand in the half-shadows. In any case, it is evident that Homer's and Johnson's work is close during this period, a closeness explained less well by parallel, independent development than by some sort of contact between them.

Late in 1866, Homer decided to visit Paris, possibly because two of his pictures, *Prisoners from the Front* and *The Bright Side*, were included in the American section at the large Universal Exposition. They were attracting favorable attention. Said the *Gazette des Beaux-Arts:* "This is firm, precise painting, in the manner of Gérôme, but with less dryness"; and the London *Art Journal:* "These works are real; the artist paints what he has seen and known."[15] Although several members of the international jury had voted to award a medal to Homer, there were not enough votes to carry it, and Frederic Church received the prize. Another attraction for Homer could have been his friend and former associate at Bufford's, J. Foxcroft Cole, who was then painting in Paris and in the country at Cerney-la-Ville. He had studied with Emile Jacques in Paris and knew other Barbizon painters at Cerney.[16]

Just whom Homer saw on his trip and what his exact movements were are unclear. Speculation has coalesced in conflicting arguments, one point of view holding that Homer "did no studying and no serious work while in Paris,"[17] another arguing "that Homer's trip to Paris was the most important event in his entire career as an artist."[18] The truth probably lies somewhere between. While in Paris he shared a studio on Montmartre with his friend from Belmont, Massachusetts, Albert W. Kelsey, who afterward recalled that Homer had "thoroughly enjoyed the life" there.[19] Evidently he did, for two drawings contributed to *Harper's* for engraving in November, 1867, were scenes of *A Parisian Ball—Dancing at the Mabille* and *Dancing at the Casino.*

But he also must have had some interest in art and artistic activities. His early work in Boston, after all, did not develop without some awareness of English painting and theory and of the American genre tradition. He at least visited the Louvre, which provided the source for one *Harper's* illustration (ILL. 2–20). Although he was not a copyist himself then, it is inconceivable that he did not look at the old masters with an artist's eye. It is also a logical supposition that he went to see the Universal Exposition, where his own pictures were hanging, and in all likelihood went to see the infamous exhibition of Manet's paintings rejected by the Exposition. In Manet's work at this time, there is much that he would have found to be similar to his own art. Although *Olympia* and the *Déjeuner sur l'Herbe* had scandalized the French public a few years earlier, Manet's flat patterning, vigorous brushwork, and strong lighting would have appealed to Homer. Some acquaintance with Manet's painting appears to explain the lighter palette in Homer's work after his return from Paris,

49

for example, *The Bridle Path, Mount Washington* of 1868 (COLOR PLATE 14); and the stronger sense of two-dimensional design, as in *Children on a Fence* of 1874 (ILL. 3–28).

Through his friend Cole he could have been introduced as well to the work of the Barbizon painters. Both *Girl with Pitchfork*, 1867 (ILL. 2–26), and *The Return of the Gleaner*, also 1867 (Collection Mrs. Homer Strong), are strongly reminiscent of Millet. For a small engraved illustration of *The Sower* in the August, 1878, issue of *Scribner's Monthly*, Homer even more patently borrowed his subject from Millet's well-known series (ILLS. 2–27 and 2–28). *Cerney la Ville—French Farm* in turn seems to derive from Corot's rural village scenes (ILLS. 2–29 and 2–30). A painter of the countryside himself, Homer would naturally have been attracted to the French nature painters; his treatment of the barn architecture and landscape stresses the play of various geometric volumes and planes in the composition in a manner close to Corot's. Both Homer's subjects and his style at this time indicate a sufficient debt to contemporary French painting to make clear that he did not spend some nine months in Paris oblivious to the contemporary art world.

In at least one instance, he actually based a picture on someone else's image, and significantly it was not another painting that he drew upon. This was his *Gargoyles of Notre Dame*, 1867, which was based on Charles Nègre's photograph of *Henry Le Secq at Notre Dame* (ILLS. 2–31 and 2–33). Working with techniques developed by the English and Scottish, Frenchmen like Louis Blanquart-Evrard, Henry Le Secq, and Charles Nègre advanced the uses of calotype photography by producing prints in bulk and thus making them available for book illustration. By the 1850's, their work was widely circulated and well known. Both Le Secq and Nègre were noted for their architectural and street views.[20] The latter's photograph, therefore, brings both men together in an important moment. It is not hard to see the connection Homer made with his own situation. In his painting, he replaces the silhouetted figure of Le Secq with a portrait of his own close friend Kelsey, who is seen brooding on the stone balcony to the right of the gargoyle. As seems likely, Homer had already become interested in contemporary photography for artistic reasons during the Civil War. He certainly used photographs later in his career, taken both by himself and his brother Charles, on fishing trips in Florida and in the Adirondacks (compare ILLS. 5–7 and 5–10). To date we have probably overlooked this kind of source material in his art because of Homer's remarkable abilities for putting his own stamp on his creative production. In the present instance, there is at least one drawing (ILL. 2–32) related to his Notre Dame picture—perhaps a preparatory study or a parody of the subject. With the Paris rooftops below, a man leans out over the railing with a wishbone to tempt a cat crouched at the end of a stone gargoyle. The absurdity of the situation and the staring expressions of man, animal, and stone face produce a comic touch uncommon in Homer's work.

Another unresolved aspect related to Homer's visit to France is the role of Japanese prints in his art. One major section of the Universal Exposition was devoted to Japanese arts and crafts. Actually, prints by artists like Hokusai (ILLS. 5–16 and 5–29) and Hiroshige had already appeared among dealers, collectors, and artists both in Europe and America before this. The Oriental vogue was to become a major one during the late nineteenth century, affecting the art of painters as diverse as Degas, van Gogh, Monet in France; Whistler and Mary Cassatt, expatriates in Europe; and Americans like John La Farge. A friend of Homer's, La Farge was collecting Japanese prints during the early 1860's and could well have interested Homer in them.[21] Unquestionably, his previous training in graphic art—his sensitivity to patterns of black and white, to linear arabesques and outlines, to asymmetrical compositional balance, and to cropping by the framing edges—would have made him naturally sympathetic to both Japanese prints and Manet's art. His work prior to the Paris trip, the *Sharp-shooter* being a notable example, had already demonstrated his initial understanding of these devices.

Several specific drawings from during and immediately after the Paris trip indicate Homer's response to Oriental subjects. For *Harper's* early in 1868, he contributed an illustration entitled *St. Valentine's Day* (ILL. 2–34), which depicts various couples, including a Japanese pair derived from the familiar prints of actors by Sharaku and others. Not long after, he drew two sketches (Cooper-Hewitt Museum, New York) of Chinese smoking opium, which were preparatory to his 1874 illustration in *Harper's, The Chinese in New York—Scene in a Baxter Street Club House* (ILL. 2–35). One of his more finished drawings in this group is *International Tea Party* (ILL. 2–36), which bears both obvious allusions to Japanese prints and less obvious relation to contemporary French painting. The relaxed seated figures, especially the rather fashionable women, recall pictures such as Manet's *Garden of the Tuileries* of 1860, Monet's *Terasse à St. Addresse* of 1866 (Metropolitan Museum, New York), and the early café scenes by Renoir. In fact, touches of Monet and Boudin continue to surface, whether consciously or unconsciously, throughout Homer's subsequent work (see COLOR PLATES 12, 20, 24, and ILL. 5–18).

Still a further connection with this group is that suggested by another 1867 painting, *Amateur Musicians*, and comparable subjects by Degas (ILLS. 2–37 and 2–38). Although Degas's painting postdates Homer's by a few years, the French artist had in the mid-1860's already begun to paint informal portraits of his family and friends in Paris. With very carefully balanced designs of picture space and surface, Degas concentrated on probing and revealing the psychological character of his sitters. Certainly Homer's painting is unquestionably French in subject, whether he found it in Degas or elsewhere during his trip. The two figures in each case are similarly framed by the sheets of music and playing instruments. Yet, there are subtle differences between them. Degas's portrait of his father listening to Pagans playing the guitar stresses the contrasts of age and action between the two men. Pagans, active, singing, is shown upright and in profile, while the artist's father is seen as more relaxed and contemplative, his silhouette appropriately quieter and more self-contained. Finally, the guitar serves both as the division and as the juncture between the two men.

Homer's painting is also one of absorption—a combination of intellectual concentration and physical activity—yet he shows little of Degas's interest in revealing the individual (or identifiable) characters of his musicians. His viewpoint is more detached and the over-all treatment more anecdotal than Degas's work. In addition, rather than the shallow composition so characteristic of French Impressionism, Homer retains his relatively deep pictorial space. However, between the expressive compositional designs employed by Degas and by Japanese prints, Homer was able to reinforce the natural direction of his own style. The Paris trip, therefore, appears to have caused no upheaval in the development of his art, although it did strengthen his work in new and decisive ways. One demonstration of this was his engraving published in *Harper's* just after his return. With its cropped diagonals, asymmetrical balance of figures and shipdeck, and tension between two- and three-dimensional design, *Homeward Bound* (ILL. 2–39) was among Homer's most original and forceful drawings to date.

2-1. *The Army of the Potomac—A Sharp-shooter on Picket Duty*, 1862. Wood engraving, 9 x 13⅝ inches. Courtesy, Trustees of Dartmouth College, Hanover, New Hampshire.

2-2. *A Bivouac Fire on the Potomac*, 1861. Wood engraving, 13¾ x 20⅛ inches. Courtesy, Trustees of Dartmouth College, Hanover, New Hampshire.

2-3. *The War for the Union, 1862—A Cavalry Charge,* 1862. Wood engraving, 13¾ x 20⅝ inches. Courtesy, Trustees of Dartmouth College, Hanover, New Hampshire.

2-4. *The Approach of the British Pirate "Alabama,"* 1863. Wood engraving, 13½ x 10 inches. Courtesy, Trustees of Dartmouth College, Hanover, New Hampshire.

Below

2-5. *Three Days on the Front*, c. 1863. Chalk on paper, 9 x 17¾ inches. Cooper-Hewitt Museum of Decorative Arts and Design, Smithsonian Institution, New York.

Right

2-6. George N. Barnard: *Confederate Fortifications, Atlanta,* 1864. Photograph, 10¼ x 14¾ inches. Private collection.

2-7. Mathew Brady: *Dead Boy in the Road at Fredericksburg*, 1863. Photograph, 8½ x 12 inches. Library of Congress.

2-8. *Wounded Soldier*, 1864. Charcoal and chalk on paper, 14⅜ x 19½ inches. Cooper-Hewitt Museum of Decorative Arts and Design, Smithsonian Institution, New York.

58

Left
2-9. Timothy O'Sullivan: *Confederate Prisoners*, 1863. Photograph, 4 x 5 inches. Library of Congress.

Above
2-10. Gustave Courbet: *Bonjour Monsieur Courbet*, 1854. Oil on canvas, 51 x 59 inches, Musée Fabre, Montpellier, France.

2-11. *Skirmish in the Wilderness*, 1864. Oil on canvas, 18 x 26 inches. The New Britain Museum of American Art, New Britain, Connecticut. Harriet Russell Stanley Fund.

Left

2-12. Albert Bierstadt: *Attack on a Union Picket Post*, 1862. Oil on canvas, 15 x 17¾ inches. The Century Association, New York. (Photograph courtesy of Frick Art Reference Library.)

Below

2-13. *The Army of the Potomac—Our Outlying Picket in the Woods*, 1862. Wood engraving, 6¾ x 19⅛ inches. Courtesy, Trustees of Dartmouth College, Hanover, New Hampshire.

Left

2-14. Eastman Johnson: *The Wounded Drummer Boy*, 1871. Oil on canvas 47¾ x 38½ inches. Union League Club of New York. (Photograph courtesy of Frick Art Reference Library.)

Above

2-15. *Cavalry Soldier on Horseback*, c. 1863. Crayon on paper, 14⅜ x 9½ inches. Cooper-Hewitt Museum of Decorative Arts and Design, Smithsonian Institution, New York.

Below

2-16. *The Letter from Home*, 1863. Lithograph, 14 x 10⅞ inches.
Philadelphia Museum of Art. Purchased: The Harrison Fund.

Right

2-17. Eastman Johnson: *The Letter Home*, 1867. Oil on panel,
23 x 27½ inches. Courtesy, Museum of Fine Arts, Boston.
M. and M. Karolik Collection.

Above

2-18. *Croquet Players*, 1865. Oil on canvas, 16 x 26 inches. Albright-Knox Art Gallery, Buffalo, New York.

Left

2-19. Claude Monet: *Women in a Garden*, 1866-67. Oil on canvas 100¼ x 81¾ inches. Musée du Louvre, Paris.

Croquet Scene, 1866. Oil on canvas, 16 x 26 inches. The Art Institute of Chicago. Friends of American Art Collection.

High Tide: The Bathers, 1870. Oil on canvas, 26 x 38 inches. The Metropolitan Museum of Art. Gift of Mrs. William F. Milton, 1923.

Waiting for Dad, 1873. Oil on canvas, 9½ x 14 inches. Collection of Mr. and Mrs. Paul Mellon.

The Morning Bell, 1866. Oil on canvas, 24 x 38¼ inches. Yale University Art Library. Bequest of Stephen Carlton Clark.

COLOR PLATE 9.
New England Country School, 1872. Oil on canvas, 12 x 18 inches. Addison Gallery of American Art,
Phillips Academy, Andover, Massachusetts.

Opposite
COLOR PLATE 10.
Snap the Whip, 1872. (Detail of Ill. 3-9.)

Above
COLOR PLATE 11.
The Dinner Horn, 1873. Oil on canvas, 12 x 14 inches. The Detroit Institute of Arts. Gift of Dexter M. Ferry, Jr.

71

COLOR PLATE 12.
Long Branch, New Jersey, 1869. Oil on canvas, 16 x 21¾ inches. Courtesy, Museum of Fine Arts, Boston. Charles Henry Hayden Fund.

Below

2-20. *Art Students and Copyists in the Louvre Gallery, Paris, 1868.* Wood engraving, 10 x 13½ inches. Courtesy, Trustees of Dartmouth College, Hanover, New Hampshire.

Right

2-21. Eastman Johnson: *Hollyhocks*, 1876. Oil on canvas, 23½ x 30¼ inches. The New Britain Museum of American Art, New Britain, Connecticut. Harriet Russell Stanley Fund.

2-22. *The Veteran in a New Field*, 1865. Oil on canvas, 24 x 38 inches. The Metropolitan Museum of Art. Bequest of Miss Adelaide Milton de Groot, 1967.

Above left

2-23. William Sidney Mount: *Farmer Whetting His Scythe*, 1848. Oil on canvas, 24 x 20 inches. Suffolk Museum and Carriage House, Melville Collection, Stony Brook, Long Island, New York.

Left

2-24. *Green Apples*, 1868. Wood engraving, 5⅞ x 3⅝ inches. Courtesy, Trustees of Dartmouth College, Hanover, New Hampshire.

Above

2-25. *Haymaking*, 1864. Oil on canvas, 16 x 11 inches. The Columbus Gallery of Fine Arts, Columbus, Ohio. Howald Fund.

Left
2-26. *Girl with Pitchfork*, 1867. Oil on canvas, 24 x 10½ inches. The Phillips Collection, Washington, D.C.

Above
2-27. *The Sower*, 1868. Wood engraving, 2⅞ x 4⅞ inches. Private collection.

Below
2-28. Jean François Millet: *The Sower*, 1850. Oil on canvas, 39¾ x 32½ inches. Courtesy, Museum of Fine Arts, Boston. Shaw Collection.

Below

2-29. *Cerney la Ville—French Farm*, 1866. Oil on panel, 10½ x 18¼ inches. Krannert Art Museum, University of Illinois, Champaign.

Right

2-30. Jean Baptiste Camille Corot: *Church at Lormes*, c. 1841. Oil on canvas, 13½ x 18¼ inches. Wadsworth Atheneum, Hartford, Connecticut. Ella Gallup Sumner and Mary Catlin Sumner Collection.

Left

2-31. Charles Nègre: *Henry Le Secq at Notre Dame Cathedral, Paris*, 1851. Calotype 12⅝ x 8⅛ inches. Collection André M. Jammes, Paris.

Below

2-32. *View of Paris*, 1867. Pen and ink and pencil on paper, 7¼ x 11⅛ inches. Cooper-Hewitt Museum of Decorative Arts and Design, Smithsonian Institution, New York.

Opposite

2-33. *Gargoyles of Notre Dame*, 1867. Oil on canvas, 19 x 13 inches. Collection of James M. Thomson.

Left

2-34. *St. Valentine's Day—The Old Story in All Lands*, 1868.
Wood engraving, 13¾ x 9⅛ inches. Courtesy, Trustees of
Dartmouth College, Hanover, New Hampshire.

Right

2-35. *The Chinese in New York—Scene in a Baxter Street Club
House*, 1874. Wood engraving, 13⅝ x 8⅞ inches. Courtesy,
Trustees of Dartmouth College, Hanover, New Hampshire.

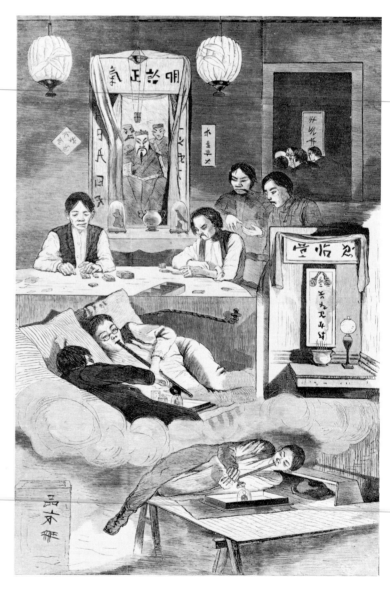

2-36. *International Tea Party*, c. 1874. Pencil and wash on paper, 8⅛ x 10⅜ inches. Cooper-Hewitt Museum of Decorative Arts and Design, Smithsonian Institution, New York.

Left
2-37. Edgar Degas: *The Artist's Father Listening to Pagans Playing the Guitar*, 1874. Oil on canvas, 32 x 25½ inches. Courtesy, Museum of Fine Arts, Boston. Bequest of John T. Spaulding.

Above
2-38. *Amateur Musicians*, 1867. Oil on canvas, 18 x 15 inches. The Metropolitan Museum of Art. Samuel D. Lee Fund, 1939.

2-39. *Homeward Bound*, 1867. Wood engraving, 10 x 13½ inches. Courtesy, Trustees of Dartmouth College, Hanover, New Hampshire.

Left
3-1. *Watching the Crows*, c. 1868. Pencil on paper, 5⅞ x 3⅝ inches. Courtesy, Museum of Fine Arts, Boston.

Above
3-2. *Watching the Crows*, 1868. Wood engraving, 5⅞ x 3⅝ inches. Courtesy, Trustees of Dartmouth College, Hanover, New Hampshire.

3

A Fresh Eye and Wholesome Independence

BACK IN NEW YORK at the end of 1867, Homer again worked extensively on illustrations, presumably in need of recovering his recent expenses. Among his engravings for *Harper's* in January, 1868, was *"Winter"—A Skating Scene,* a strongly patterned print of a familiar subject. To *Our Young Folks* he contributed between 1867 and 1868 a smaller series of engravings of young boys and girls in the fields, some swinging on a birch tree, others catching birds in a hay field, watching for crows, picking strawberries or green apples (ILLS. 2–24 and 3–1). He also submitted illustrations to *Galaxy, Appleton's Journal, Hearth and Home,* and to the Boston publication *Every Saturday.* Book illustration interested him at this time as well, and drawings by him appeared in volumes by Whittier, Longfellow, Lowell, Bryant, and Tennyson. At the same time, he was beginning to explore the more complex relationship between his oils, drawings, and engravings. He was discovering distinctive aspects in the character of each medium, for example, how light is rendered, forms are defined, or figures and landscape related. In the summer of 1868 he did an oil of *The Bridle Path, Mount Washington* (COLOR PLATE 14) showing a young lady on horseback near the summit. Soon after, he painted another picture of the same girl (Chicago Art Institute) now seen with a friend and larger group of horses. The composition finally evolved into yet another arrangement of the figures and horses on the mountainside in an engraving that appeared in *Harper's* (ILL. 3–3) the following summer.

The subjects of these years, children and wistful young women, were the ones he would draw and paint repeatedly during the next decade. At the same time, his work was not without stylistic experimentation, as demonstrated by *High Tide: The Bathers,* painted in 1870 (COLOR PLATE 6). Compared to some of his other oils, this possesses an unusual tightness and hardness of form, perhaps derived from his style of work in engravings. The long shadows, the two hidden faces, the unsure reaction of the dog, the strange pale green of the water, and the otherwise empty beach intimate an almost disquieting stillness in the scene. Of this and other paintings from that year one contemporary critic wrote:

> The pictures are not wholly pleasing; perhaps the bathing scene—like another which he has in the east room—is not quite refined. But the pictures show a fresh eye and a wholesome independence of conventions with spirit and vigor.[1]

The sculpturesque quality of the figures enhances the mood of seriousness which Homer has created. The ambivalence that seems to exist between this seriousness and ordinary anecdotal genre is never fully explained. Could the reason lie in the identity of the girl seated on the beach—said by the family to be the one love of his lifetime? Homer is as reticent here as he was in the only other picture thought to have been of this special girl in his personal life. Entitled "*Shall I Tell Your Fortune?*" it depicted her seated on the grass with a hand of cards and facing the viewer to ask her question. The painting remained on an easel in Homer's studio throughout his later years.[2] We shall probably never know the full substance of his relationship with this girl, or for that matter his general attitudes toward the opposite sex. Even in his most sympathetic pictures of young women, their femininity seems to be more part of a mood than an intimately felt characteristic. After the 1870's, he saw women less and less, except for Charles's wife, Mattie, who remained close to him for the rest of his life. But like most matters in his private life, this one, as he replied to Downes, was "of no concern to the public," and we are left only with our own speculations.

At this time, he also undertook several pictures of the leisurely and fashionable life at the resorts on the mid-Atlantic coast. The best known of these is *Long Branch, New Jersey*, 1869, which he reworked in an engraving for *Harper's* the following year (COLOR PLATE 12 and ILL. 3–4). The style and subject matter of the early Monet and Boudin (ILLS. 2–19 and 4–3) are now even stronger, although Homer retains that American sense of solidly modeled forms and deep spatial recession. While these fashionable ladies with parasols and billowing skirts echo those promenading on the Channel beaches in contemporary French painting, Homer consciously leads the eye from the sharply defined foreground platform toward the distant horizon. Unlike Monet's rather flattened garden path, here the edge of the cliff, the diagonally receding walkway, and the noticeable change in figure scale assist in maintaining the deep pictorial space.

The heightened sense in his engraving *On the Bluff at Long Branch, at the Bathing Hour* of cropped forms at the edges, crisp linear and tonal patterns, as well as the strong visual tension between two- and three-dimensional organization of shapes, reflect his confident absorption of the stylistic devices to be found in Japanese prints and French painting. Not surprisingly, this plein-air style appears at just about the same time in Johnson's work. Perhaps under Homer's stimulus, Johnson also began a series of similar pictures, mostly painted on Nantucket Island through the 1870's. One undated oil of a *Woman on a Hill* (ILL. 3–5) is almost an exact copy of the central figure in Homer's painting of Long Branch. The summary picture of Johnson's series came in 1880 with *The Cranberry Harvest, Island of Nantucket* (ILL. 3–6). There the carefully balanced arrangement of figures in space, the central standing woman, the bright coloring and crisp detailing, the strong receding diagonal of the hillside at once echo Homer's painting while also establishing Johnson as a master in his own right.

If Johnson's Nantucket pictures may have been painted with an eye on Homer's style, there is stylistic evidence to suggest that, in turn, Homer was equally conscious of Johnson's art. In 1871, Johnson had painted *The Old Stage Coach* (ILL. 3–7); at about the same time another mutual friend, Enoch Wood Perry, painted *The Departure of the Pemigewasset Coach* (ILL. 3–8). Were the happily gesturing and running boys, the generally lateral organization of forms in these two pictures the inspiration for Homer's *Snap the Whip* (ILLS. 3–9, 3–10, and 3–12)? The three artists were close friends in New York,[3] and the closeness in time and style of these paintings seems more logical than coincidental. Certain details of Johnson's picture derive from his Düsseldorf training, notably the rather tight drawing and the elaborately waving figure atop the coach, who seems to have stepped (along with George Caleb Bingham's dancing figure in his *Jolly Flatboatmen* series) out of Emmanuel Leutze's *Westward the Course of Empire Takes Its Way*. But the central four figures in Homer's line of boys is close indeed to Johnson's four at the left, who are pretending to pull the coach.

Homer's first drawings for *Snap the Whip* (ILL. 3–10) showed the central group of boys more tightly interlocked than they are in the final painting. In a small oil study (COLOR PLATE 10 and ILL. 3–9), the figures are more spread out laterally across the composition, allowing for greater clarity of each figure and a rhythmic play of silhouette among them. Homer made one other major change between this and the final version (ILL. 3–12), namely the addition of the mountainscape in the background. While he may have done this with the prints of Hokusai (ILL. 5–16) in mind, the slope of the distant hillside serves the important purpose of framing the action in the foreground: Its gentle slope at once echoes both the line of boys and the roof of the red schoolhouse, which was the subject of yet another oil study (ILL. 3–11). Paradoxically, the hillside both closes in the space and establishes another layer in depth, after the figures and the schoolhouse building.

These are ultimately images of sheer joy and optimism, although Homer was not without a tempering sense of seriousness and discipline. This was evident in another picture of this year, *New England Country School* (COLOR PLATE 9), which presumably depicts the inside of the schoolhouse seen in *Snap the Whip*. The deceptively simple composition subtly plays off symmetry and asymmetry: The teacher stands at the center of the canvas but slightly to the right of the center of the blackboard; the walls and benches seem to recede equally in from the corners, but clearly they do not; the view of

A FRESH EYE AND WHOLESOME INDEPENDENCE

the desk is seemingly both frontal and three-quarters. Moreover, the picture presents one of Homer's most complex, yet legible, arrangements of linear and planar forms, which include the windows, blackboard, walls, benches and desk. Yet, the strong architectural structure of the design, both metaphorically and literally, remains a setting for the human element, and the final resolution of the picture is its spare equilibrium between animate and inanimate, the figures and architectural furniture. Thus, the very design of the picture complements the sense of simple but strong virtues, such as orderly, pragmatic learning, and the essential meaning of the one-room schoolhouse.

As was frequently the case in these years, Homer made a variant design of the picture for a *Harper's* engraving, which appeared in 1873 as *The Noon Recess* (ILL. 3-13). Now taking only a corner of the room, he showed the teacher and one student doing makeup reading. Another related work was *Homework* (ILL. 3-15), a small watercolor of a youth reading at his desk beneath an open window. In some cases, Homer reversed the process of working from oil to engraving. In *The Dinner Horn*, for example, the engraving appeared in 1870 and served as the basis for an oil completed three years later (ILL. 3-14 and COLOR PLATE 11). Here Homer moved the figure of the woman blowing the horn from outside the house to a covered porch. Clearly, he enjoyed the variations in composition and execution as he moved back and forth between the two media. Yet in other cases he made almost no changes at all, as in *Waiting for Dad* (COLOR PLATE 7) and its companion engraving, *"Dad's Coming,"* both of which were done in 1873. This is one of his sparest and most expressive designs. The sculptural and immobile figures recall those in *High Tide* (COLOR PLATE 6) of a few years before, and convey a similar sense of gravity. These occasional moods of more serious substance counterpoint the otherwise carefree subject matter of this period and perhaps indicate the direction his art would take in the next decade.

Children at play or rest were a favorite subject of Homer's throughout the 1870's. In 1873, he spent his first summer painting in Gloucester, Massachusetts, and the next year he went to the Adirondacks. In these spots and elsewhere, he worked on several related pictures of youths seated on rocks or in fields under the summer sun (ILLS. 3-16 to 3-19 and COLOR PLATE 13). His drawings were quick outline sketches of various postures or compositional arrangements. Some were tentative efforts to relate the figures to the setting, and one of his frequent devices was to echo the number of heads with usually the same number of sailboats positioned on the horizon behind them. In other instances, the drawings possess an almost abstract rhythm of their own in the placement of figures across the bare sheet of paper (ILLS. 3-18 and 3-19). This habit of swiftly sketching several figures or heads from slightly different points of view was one that Homer had developed during the Civil War in drawing the features or movements of soldiers. These drawings then became the raw material for subsequent oil paintings, as is evident with pictures like *The Nooning* and *Boys in a Pasture* (COLOR PLATE 13, ILLS. 3-16 and 3-17). These are small oils painted with bright colors of yellows and greens and filled with glowing sunlight, which radiates a sense of intimate warmth and optimism.

Homer included additional figures and a line of laundry in his engraving of the latter subject (ILL. 3–21). One senses these changes were a response in part to the basically tonal patterns inherent in using the graphic medium and in part to the more narrative requirements of magazine illustration. Whereas the added boys in the foreground and the woman feeding chickens in the left background give the engraving its own narrative character, the oil possesses a special quality of contemplation and calm. It is a mistake to read such pictures by Homer as merely charming genre pieces of youthful pastimes and pleasures, because the frequent tone of revery also intimates a more profound awareness of time and mortality. Such subjects for Homer were, in fact, studies of the meaning of youth: its suspension and poise in the transition of growing up.

During the early 1870's, Homer began to compose his paintings with increasing sophistication, regularly employing the background forms of the landscape or buildings to frame the primary figures in the foreground. This manner of composing, as well as the delight in youthful outdoor pursuits, may conceivably have been stimulated by the popular genre pictures of William Sidney Mount. That Homer may have earlier taken note of Mount's work has already been suggested. Furthermore, Eastman Johnson's early oils show the influence of Mount. The latter's barn-dancing series seems to be the direct prototype for *Old Kentucky Home, Life in the South* (Metropolitan Museum, New York) by Johnson; and Mount's *Power of Music* of 1858 specifically seems to have affected the composition of Johnson's *Corn Husking* of 1860 (Syracuse Museum of Fine Arts, Syracuse, New York). Mount's mature works all display his distinctive taste for counterpointing his figures with nearby architectural or landscape forms. For example, in *Bargaining for a Horse* (New-York Historical Society), he frames the central characters and horse with the vertical and horizontal slats of a fence behind them. Homer could have readily known the engraving after this work or seen Mount's original oils directly in New York galleries.

One of Mount's most characteristic works is *Cider Making*, 1851 (ILL. 3–20), and it shows well how he carefully groups his figures. In threes or fours, each group is placed next to some architectural or landscape form: the children in the foreground next to the barrels, those behind on the apple-crushing wheel (and framed by the hillside beyond), the men beneath the cider-mill roof, and Mount himself with two companions in the right distance standing in front of a covered haystack. Each of these is, of course, a separate anecdotal moment, associated as a sequence in time with one another. Homer's mode of picture-making in the 1870's is strikingly similar; even his sense of the happy union between youth and nature, the optimistic plenitude of sunlight, the ripeness of summer's fruit are themes first articulated by Mount.

Another possible influence in the choice and treatment of his subjects at this time may have been Fitz Hugh Lane's paintings of Gloucester, which were frequently on view at the Boston Athenaeum and at Chester Harding's gallery. If there was some connection between Lane's and Homer's illustrations for music-sheet covers, as seems likely, there is good reason to believe that Homer also was acquainted with Lane's successful oil paintings. Often Lane included in the foregrounds of his views one or two youths looking across the harborscape (ILL. 3–22). Lane's contemplation and quiet celebration of nature would have held a natural appeal for Homer. But where Lane preferred the detached and distant viewpoint, Homer chose to move in closer and more intimately on his subject.

Homer spent his first summer in Gloucester in 1873, and this coincided with another important development in his artistic career—the taking up of watercolor. Unlike oil, this new medium was fluid and transparent. It permitted quick and improvisory sketching in color directly out-of-doors and thus offered a means of expression that was somewhere between black-and-white drawing and oil painting. Watercolors in America up to this time were primarily color drawings, often of topographical or scientific subjects. Among Homer's great contributions to American art was the transformation of this medium from its more limited descriptive functions to an art form expressive in its own right. His own early watercolors are relatively tight, not yet fully liberated from colored drawings, but steadily they became freer and more expressive of the medium's special potentialities. Those of 1873 are usually filled with a number of figures engaged in happy chores near the beach or wharves.

Boys Wading and *A Basket of Clams* (ILL. 3–23 and COLOR PLATE 15) are typical. Already the freedom in rendering details and the openness of the design indicate Homer's realization of the possibilities of watercolor. For one thing, the use of the white sheet itself was especially suitable to capturing the effects of bright sunlight, and increasingly Homer left areas of the page untouched or only thinly washed to render different intensities of light. Particularly interesting in these works is the pictorial organization, so reminiscent of Mount's style. In *Boys Wading*, for instance, Homer intentionally echoes the two figures with the cropped masts of the schooner behind them and the dock cranes in the right distance. Similarly, both the pair of masts and booms frame the two boys in *A Basket of Clams*. Homer combined this latter watercolor with another of a different group having a clambake to produce the more complex composition of his engraving on the same subject (ILLS. 3–24 and 3–25). The pair of boys was a grouping that must have particularly appealed to Homer, for he continued to reuse the figuration in later, quite different pictures, such as *Cotton Pickers*, 1876 (Collection Mr. and Mrs. James Cox Brady); *Going Berrying*, 1879 (ILL. 3–26); and *Two Girls on the Beach, Tynemouth*, 1881 (Collection Mrs. John S. Ames).

Homer was at his best in this period with only a couple or small group of figures. He enjoyed pairing a boy and a girl seated on a plow (ILL. 3–27), swinging on a swing, or climbing on a fence. In each instance he subtly played them off against the surrounding lines or forms, usually also isolated in similar pairs or framing parallels. These devices permeated all media—drawings, watercolors, and oils. Among the more notable in the latter group are

Gloucester Farm of 1874 and *Weaning the Calf* of 1875 (COLOR PLATE 17 and ILL. 3–29). Choosing a low vantage point in the former, Homer sets off the two heads above the horizon of the hillside, silhouetting one against the sky and the other against the barn. In turn he juxtaposes the pair with the two grazing cows at the left and the two farmhouse roofs at the right. Like Mount's *Cider Making*, *Weaning the Calf* is also a series of incidents, here arranged in related pairs: the boy and the calf, two watching youths, a pair of roosters, another figure with the cow, all framed by the two trees and haystacks.

These thoughtfully conceived and executed pictorial constructions made 1873 a remarkably productive year for Homer. The adjustments and variations he was making in his compositions were reflected in the number that resulted in engravings for *Harper's*. Among the illustrations that were combinations of several previous drawings or watercolors was *Gloucester Harbor*, based on two related watercolors of boys rowing in the harbor, and *Ship Building, Gloucester*, which combines no less than three other works (ILLS. 3–30, 3–31, 3–34, and 3–35). Each of these earlier images, done over a two-year period, is obviously a picture of a separately observed activity. All possess a quiet and unpretentious gravity. *The Boat Builders* has a particularly unassuming simplicity and force. Successfully balanced are the two boys and the rocks, the shapes of their hats and their boats, and the one toy boat seen juxtaposed to the distant sailing vessel on the horizon. (Another adept touch is the abstract shape of the boy's hat casting its shadow on his sails.) The unobtrusive relationship between the two scales of sailboats led Homer to the more obvious combination of both boys and men building their boats on the Gloucester wharves. It is interesting to consider the subtle changes he made between the first pictures and the final engraved illustration. For example, the repeated pilings above the heads of the figures in *Boys on a Beach* prompted him to silhouette more the railings on the large boat in his engraving, while the piles of planking and beams on the ground in the oil of *Ship Building* serve as transitional shapes between foreground figures and background vessel in the final print. Thus, visual design again helps to reinforce the two joined worlds of shipmaking depicted here.

By the time Homer came to paint in Gloucester, Cape Ann had become a popular summer resort. Already in the 1850's, advertisements in the Boston papers celebrated its rural carriageways, seashore vistas, and commodious hotels. Lane painted Gloucester in the 1850's and early 60's as the city rose to new prosperity from fishing and shipping. Although summer houses were going up along its shores, much of Cape Ann continued to retain its pastoral solitude, attracting painters like Martin Johnson Heade and Alfred T. Bricher. Contemporary with Homer in Gloucester was William Morris Hunt, who painted his picture of the harbor (ILL. 3–32) in 1877. Most artists painting in Gloucester have responded to its rugged coastline—the small coves and rocky ledges—and common to their work is an acute awareness of light.[4] Although Hunt's style obviously differs from Homer's, there is a shared attention to sunlight as the primary animating reality of their paintings.

Hunt also had a solid New England background but spent a good deal more time abroad than did Homer. Hunt went first to Rome for study and then during the 1850's to Düsseldorf. He was back in Boston by the early 1870's, highly successful as a fashionable and accomplished portraitist. After his studio burned in 1872, he took to traveling more in the country to paint. The summer of 1877 found him settled at Kettle Cove on Cape Ann, where he began his painting of Gloucester harbor. Painted in one day on the spot, it was the first picture in which he felt he had captured a convincing sense of outdoor light.[5] Indeed, light or its reflections and shadows fill the canvas, defining, softening, and dissolving forms. The quick, fluid brushwork and the bright palette clearly indicate that Hunt was setting his impressions down directly from nature. But his more painterly style was essentially closer to European sources—such as the landscapes of the Barbizon and early Impressionist painters —than to the tighter draftsmanship and solidly defined forms of Homer's art. This alternative manner of Hunt's would continue in the sparkling Gloucester views of Childe Hassam's at the end of the century.

For Homer at this time, figures still played an important role in his paintings, and among his summary (and best-known) oils of this period is *Breezing Up* (COLOR PLATE 19), also known as *A Fair Wind*. Shown at the National Academy exhibition of 1876, it was characterized as "the author's greatest hit since the 'Confederate Prisoners.'"[6] With bright touches of brushwork, lively coloring, and an animated design, the picture perfectly embodies the excitement of boys out for an afternoon's sail. The theme of boys having fun on their own was a popular one in American art and literature at this time. Such youths became projections of a comic abandon and naïve truthfulness that seemed missing in the adult Victorian world of the Brown Decades. They are the heroes of stories by Charles Dudley Warner and Mark Twain, and the subjects for numerous artists, including Eastman Johnson, J. G. Brown, and James Clonney. It is significant that Homer painted *Breezing Up* the same year that Twain published *Huckleberry Finn*. These works were by artists concerned, on the surface, with humor but, beneath, with serious truths. As such, they tell us something about American life in the era of Ulysses S. Grant as well as something more profound about the human condition. Homer sees the joy, innocence, and honesty of childhood as lasting human qualities, which do not have to disappear with the passing of youth.

This is why Homer's picture is an image of individual youths and of the nature of youth itself. He conveys these sentiments through devices like the jagged silhouette of the boys and man in the cockpit and the diagonal positioning of the boat. These lend a sense of active movement appropriate to the subject. In fact, in the preparatory watercolor for the painting, called *Sailing the Catboat* (COLOR PLATE 18), Homer drew a lighthouse (probably that on Eastern Point, Gloucester) in the right distance; this he replaced with a schooner under full sail, and by having it sail off in a parallel direction, he reinforces the sense of motion in the foreground. Yet, he fully invites the spectator to participate visually in the action, first, by showing the cockpit full of figures open to our view, and second, by leading the eye directly into the central activity by means of the strong diagonal of the mast and sail cutting sharply in from the upper left. Homer evidently enjoyed sailing around the Cape Ann area—he also did another drawing of a man alone in the cockpit of his sailboat off Annisquam (Cooper-Hewitt Museum, New York)—and the liberation from shore and from people must have been at once physical and spiritual.

There are also interesting parallels with such works and Thomas Eakins's sailing scenes (ILL. 3–33) of the same years. Whether there was any exchange of influences between the two artists at this time is unknown; the only documented occasion when the two men met was when they served together on the Carnegie Institute jury in 1901.[7] But in the mid 1870's, the two painters were equally concerned with the physical and metaphysical presence of light. Eakins's paintings, however, were already fundamentally portraits; Homer's figures, on the other hand, although doubtless drawn from identifiable individuals, become generalized in his picture, while Eakins's subjects emphatically retain their individuality. One even turns back to fix his glance directly at the viewer. Eakins's scientific training in mathematics, perspective, and photography also creates here a much more spatially and temporally precise image. While both artists share a similar theme in their art, subtle differences indicate the directions each man was taking. For Eakins, it was to be an understanding of humanity through individuality; for Homer, that humanity was reached through generalization and ultimately transcendence of individuality.

With the gradual success of his watercolors, the regular exhibition of his works at the National Academy and elsewhere, and the slowly increasing prices paid for his pictures, Homer could now afford to give up illustration work entirely, and so in 1874 a long and productive association with *Harper's* ended. By the mid-1870's, he was trying his hand at other subjects besides carefree children. He devoted a number of watercolors and oils between 1874 and 1880 to young women, often walking wistfully alone in the woods, picking or holding flowers, or lost in gentle revery. Examples like *Morning Glories* of 1873 (ILL. 3–39), *The Sick Chicken* (ILL. 3–38), *Hunting for Eggs, Summer* (both Clark Art Institute, Williamstown, Mass.), *In the Garden* (COLOR PLATE 20)—all from 1874— *Autumn* (Collection of Mr. and Mrs. Paul Mellon) and *The New Novel* (COLOR PLATE 21) from 1877, *Bo-Peep* (ILL. 3–37) of 1878, and *Woman with Flower* of 1880 (ILL. 3–36) are delicate in coloring, with a gentleness of effect suitable to the feminine subject matter. These are recognizable but generalized individuals, painted without idealization or sensuality. Rather, one senses a quiet and contemplative charm that again suggests Homer's preoccupation with the suspension beyond time of a special age, in this case the fullness of beauty in pretty young women. In some subconscious way, too, these pictures may also have been the artist's final valentines to the opposite sex before withdrawing into greater detachment and solitude during his later career.

The late 1870's for Homer saw several other fresh directions in his work. In 1876, he found new subjects among the blacks of rural Virginia and huntsmen in the Adirondacks, and a year later he briefly took up painting on ceramic tiles. *The Two Guides* (ILL. 3–42)

A FRESH EYE AND WHOLESOME INDEPENDENCE

was one of the first of many Adirondack scenes to be painted by Homer. Usually with his brother Charles, he had gone to upstate New York as early as 1870 to hunt and fish and to paint; in the next few years, they returned several times. The bright colors and atmospheric effects of this picture match its marine counterpart in *Breezing Up*, though in this mountainous setting there is a subtly stronger sense of man's rugged and comfortable isolation in nature. The clear juxtaposition of foreground and distant mountain vista recalls Hokusai's prints, which conceivably could have been in Homer's mind when composing this.

From a trip during 1875 to Petersburg, Virginia, Homer produced a number of oils of life among the blacks, which may be seen as southern counterparts to his Gloucester scenes. Pictures like *Watermelon Boys* (ILL. 3–43), *Sunday Morning in Virginia* (Cincinnati Art Museum), *Upland Cotton* (private collection), and *The Carnival* (COLOR PLATE 22 and ILL. 3–40) demonstrated Homer's sympathy for the color and gaiety in the lives of these individuals. These are solidly composed paintings, and the figures are often sculptural and monumental. Homer especially enjoyed the bright patterns made by the dark skin and colorful clothing of these figures. Whether at rest or play, they convey the same sense of enjoyment and self-possession as their northern contemporaries painted by Homer. In deft balance, too, are the same comic and serious touches. It is significant that *Upland Cotton* was compared to Japanese art by a reviewer of the Academy exhibition of 1879; it was, he said,

> a remarkable penetration of Japanese thought into American expression. . . . The picture is a superb piece of decoration, with its deep, queer colors like the Japanese, dull greens, dim reds, and strange, neutral blues and pinks. Japanese Art is not gorgeous, like the Turkish and Persian, but its peculiar and artistic subtlety has been assimilated precisely by Mr. Homer. This picture seems to us original and important as an example of new thought.[8]

Just as *The Two Guides* looks forward to the many north woods watercolors of Homer's later years, so these Virginia paintings anticipate the brilliant watercolors of the Caribbean (ILLS. 5–12 and 5–15).

One unusual detour in Homer's career that was little related to what preceded or followed it was his painting of tiles and participation in the Tile Club, of which he was a cofounder in 1877. Others in the group included the architect Stanford White, the sculptor Augustus Saint-Gaudens, the illustrators Edwin Austin Abbey and A. B. Frost, the painters William Merritt Chase, J. Alden Weir, and John Twachtman, and the critic Earl Shinn. Membership fluctuated during the ten years of activity between a dozen and thirty individuals. An entertaining account of the group appeared in *Scribner's Monthly* for January, 1879, which began: " 'This is a decorative age,' said an artist. 'We should do something decorative, if we should not be behind the times.' "[9] Initially, they part facetiously thought of making money by decorating tiles, but the principal pastime was regular convocations of good company and conversation.[10] Each man had a nickname within the group; Homer's was the "Obtuse Bard." He was the host for the association's first annual dinner, which was described by one present as "one of the most crisp and toasty affairs that ever took place since the time of Lucullus, involving, as it did, too, a singularly small consideration in cash *per capita*."[11] Members worked at a long table together, not taking their tile work quite as seriously as their other work, but a large number of tiles uniformly eight inches square were produced. Homer finished two sets for fireplaces in 1878, one pairing a shepherd and shepherdess on a hillside standing either side of the hearth (ILL. 3–41). Simple in design, they nonetheless show a sensitivity to given shape and their upright staffs nicely complement the narrow panel of tiles.

The group enjoyed itself enormously, taking excursions to eastern Long Island and, during the summer of 1879, an elaborate river and canal ride up the Hudson to Lake Champlain. They cooked huge feasts for themselves, and for a time in the early 1880's established headquarters in a West Tenth Street studio. While the production of tiles was an uneven affair both numerically and qualitatively, each artist may be recognized by his own style, and some examples are particularly attractive. For Homer, these must have been happy and outgoing years. Although he was soon to withdraw to the coast of Maine and to the private life of his painting, his subjects of this period were expressions of grace and well-being; his activities with friends and associates were enthusiastic and apparently unreserved. But he was in his forties now and his own youth was over; both he and his art had come to maturity. By the end of the 1870's, there are hints in his work of searches for a new style and subject matter.

He did return to Gloucester in the summer of 1880, this time establishing himself on Ten Pound Island in the harbor. This act of separation was important, for it permitted him a new solitude and freedom of action. His watercolors of this period, such as *Children Playing Under a Gloucester Wharf*, *Green Dory*, *Boy and Fallen Tree* (COLOR PLATE 23, ILLS. 3–44 and 3–45), and *Gloucester Harbor and Dory* (Fogg Art Museum, Cambridge, Mass.), display a new freshness of execution and openness of composition. He had now fully mastered the fluid and improvisory nature of the medium and worked quickly out-of-doors in the bright sunlight. The application of his washes is broader and more confident than in his previous watercolors. The less cluttered designs and more detached viewpoints of these pictures reflect Homer's increasing thoughtfulness about his art. Gradually disappearing are the concentrated narrative or anecdotal aspects of his earlier work, to be replaced by a greater interest in formal matters, on the one hand, and more serious, even philosophical, subject matter, on the other.

Criticism of Homer's work, though generally favorable and sometimes enthusiastic, continued to be mixed. Henry James wrote one of the more provocative and insightful, if not always complimentary or understanding, pieces:

> Mr. Homer goes in, as the phrase is, for perfect realism, and cares not a jot for such fantastic hair-splitting as the distinction between beauty and ugliness. He is a genuine painter; that is, to see, and to reproduce what he sees, is his only care; to think, to imagine, to select, to refine, to com-

A FRESH EYE AND WHOLESOME INDEPENDENCE

pose, to drop into any of the intellectual tricks with which other people sometimes try to eke out the dull pictorial vision—all this Mr. Homer triumphantly avoids. He not only has no imagination, but he contrives to elevate this rather blighting negative into a blooming and honorable positive. He is almost barbarously simple, and, to our eye, he is horribly ugly; but there is nevertheless something one likes about him. What is it? For ourselves, it is not his subjects. We frankly confess that we detest his subjects—his barren plank fences, his glaring, bald, blue skies, his big, dreary, vacant lots of meadows, his freckled, straight-haired Yankee urchins, his flat-breasted maidens, suggestive of a dish of rural doughnuts and pie, his calico sun-bonnets, his flannel shirts, his cowhide boots. He has chosen the least pictorial features of the least pictorial range of scenery and civilization; he has resolutely treated them as if they *were* pictorial, as if they were every inch as good as Capri or Tangiers; and, to reward his audacity, he has incontestably succeeded. It makes one feel the value of consistency; it is a proof that if you will only be doggedly literal, though you may often be unpleasing, you will at least have a stamp of your own. Mr. Homer has the great merit, moreover, that he naturally sees everything at one with its envelope of light and air. He sees not in lines, but in masses, in gross, broad masses. Things come already modelled to his eye. If his masses were only sometimes a trifly more broken, and his brush a good deal richer—if it had a good many more secrets and mysteries and coquetries, he would be, with his vigorous way of looking and seeing, even if fancy in the matter remained the same dead blank, an almost distinguished painter. In its suggestion of this blankness of fancy the picture of the young farmer flirting with the pie-nurtured maiden in the wheat field is really an intellectual curiosity. The want of grace, of intellectual detail, of reflected light, could hardly go further; but the picture was its author's best contribution, and a very honest, and vivid, and manly piece of work. Our only complaint with it is that it is damnably ugly![12]

By the end of the 1870's, Homer had reached a watershed in his life and his art. Again he decided to journey abroad, this time to England. He left in the spring of 1881 and remained away for a year and a half, during which time profound changes took place in his approach to painting. His art broadened and deepened in meaning. He discovered he could paint with even greater force. The result was an important turning point in his career, which set the stage for the major pictures of the coming years.

3-4. *On the Bluff at Long Branch, at the Bathing Hour*, 1870. Wood engraving, 10 x 13½ inches. Courtesy, Trustees of Dartmouth College, Hanover, New Hampshire.

Right

3-5. Eastman Johnson: *Woman on a Hill*, c. 1875. Oil on panel, 25½ x 21¼ inches. Addison Gallery of American Art, Phillips Academy, Andover, Massachusetts.

Below

3-6. Eastman Johnson: *The Cranberry Harvest, Island of Nantucket*, 1880. Oil on canvas, 27¼ x 54½ inches. Vose Galleries, Boston.

3-7. Eastman Johnson: *The Old Stage Coach*, 1871. Oil on canvas, 25 x 31 inches. Layton Art Gallery Collection, Milwaukee Art Center, Milwaukee.

3-8. Enoch Wood Perry: *The Pemigewasset Coach*, c. 1869. Oil on canvas, 42½ x 66¼ inches. Courtesy, Webb Gallery of American Art, Shelburne Museum, Inc., Shelburne, Vermont.

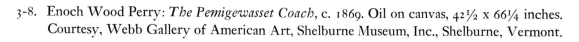

Above

3-9. *Snap the Whip*, 1872. Oil on canvas, 12 x 20
inches. The Metropolitan Museum of Art.
Gift of Christian A. Zabriskie, 1950.

Right

3-10. *Snap the Whip*, c. 1872. Chalk on paper,
9¼ x 16½ inches. Cooper-Hewitt Museum
of Decorative Arts and Design, Smithsonian
Institution, New York.

3-11. *School Time*, c. 1874. Oil on panel, 12½ x 19¼ inches. Collection of Mr. and Mrs. Paul Mellon.

3-12. *Snap the Whip*, 1872. Oil on canvas, 22 x 36 inches. Butler Institute of American Art, Youngstown, Ohio.

3-13. *The Noon Recess*, 1873. Wood engraving, 10 x 13½ inches. Courtesy, Trustees of Dartmouth College, Hanover, New Hampshire.

Above

3-14. *The Dinner Horn*, 1870. Wood engraving, 13½ x 10 inches. Courtesy, Trustees of Dartmouth College, Hanover, New Hampshire.

Opposite

3-15. *Homework*, 1874. Watercolor, 8 x 5 inches. Canajoharie Library and Art Gallery, Canajoharie, New York.

Below

3-16. *Boys in a Pasture*, 1874. Oil on canvas, 15½ x 22½ inches. Courtesy, Museum of Fine Arts, Boston. Charles Henry Hayden Fund.

Right

3-17. *The Nooning*, c. 1872. Oil on canvas, 13 x 19½ inches. Courtesy, Wadsworth Atheneum, Hartford, Connecticut. Ella Gallup Sumner and Mary Catlin Sumner Collection.

3-18. *Five Sketches of Young Boys*, c. 1872. Crayon on paper, 10⅝ x 18⅛ inches. Cooper-Hewitt Museum of Decorative Arts and Design, Smithsonian Institution, New York.

3-19. *Three Boys on a Beached Dory*, c. 1873. Pencil on paper, 7⅞ x 15½ inches. Courtesy, Museum of Fine Arts, Boston. Bequest of Estate of Katharine Dexter McCormick.

Left

3-20. William Sidney Mount: *Cider Making*, 1851. Oil on canvas, 27 x 34⅛ inches. The Metropolitan Museum of Art. Charles Allen Munn Bequest, 1966.

Below

3-21. *The Nooning*, 1873. Wood engraving, 9 x 13⅝ inches. Courtesy, Trustees of Dartmouth College, Hanover, New Hampshire.

Left

3-22. Fitz Hugh Lane: *Gloucester Harbor from Rocky Neck*, 1844. Oil on canvas, 29½ x 41½ inches. Cape Ann Historical Association, Gloucester, Massachusetts.

Below

3-23. *Boys Wading*, 1873. Watercolor, 9¼ x 13⅛ inches. Colby College Art Museum, Waterville, Maine. Harold T. Pulsifer Memorial Collection.

3-24. *The Clambake*, 1873. Watercolor, 8⅜ x 13⅞ inches. The Cleveland Museum of Art. Mrs. Homer H. Johnson Collection.

Above

3-25. *Seaside Sketches—A Clambake*, 1873. Wood engraving, 9½ x 13½ inches. Courtesy, Trustees of Dartmouth College, Hanover, New Hampshire.

Above right

3-26. *Going Berrying*, 1879. Watercolor, 8¼ x 13⅛ inches. Courtesy, Museum of Fine Arts, Boston. Bequest of Estate of Katharine Dexter McCormick.

Right

3-27. *Girl and Boy Sitting on a Plow*, 1879. Pencil on paper, 8¼ x 10½ inches. Cooper-Hewitt Museum of Decorative Arts and Design, Smithsonian Institution, New York.

113

Left
3-28. *Children on a Fence*, 1874. Watercolor, 6¾ x 11½ inches. Williams College Museum of Art, Williamstown, Massachusetts.

Below
3-29. *Weaning the Calf*, 1875. Oil on canvas, 29 x 38 inches. North Carolina Museum of Art, Raleigh.

114

3-30. *Boys on a Beach*, c. 1873. Pencil and watercolor on paper, 5½ x 13½ inches. John Davis Hatch Collection of Drawings by American Artists, Lenox, Massachusetts.

3-31. *The Boat Builders*, 1873. Oil on panel, 6 x 10¼ inches. Indianapolis Museum of Art. Martha Delzell Memorial Fund.

3-32. William Morris Hunt: *Gloucester Harbor*, 1877. Oil on canvas, 21 x 31¼ inches. Courtesy, Museum of Fine Arts, Boston. Gift of H. Nelson Slater, Mrs. Esther Slater Kerrigan, and Mrs. Ray Slater Murphy, in memory of their mother, Mabel Hunt Slater.

Below
3-33. Thomas Eakins: *Starting out After Rail*, 1874. Oil on canvas, 24 x 20 inches. Courtesy, Museum of Fine Arts, Boston. Charles Henry Hayden Fund.

Right

3-34. *Ship Building, Gloucester Harbor*, 1873. Wood engraving, 9⅛ x 13⅜ inches. Courtesy, Trustees of Dartmouth College, Hanover, New Hampshire.

Below

3-35. *Ship Building at Gloucester*, 1871. Oil on canvas, 13½ x 19¾ inches. Smith College Museum of Art, Northampton, Massachusetts.

Left

3-36. *Woman with Flower*, 1880. Watercolor, 9 x 11½ inches. Collection of Mr. and Mrs. Arthur G. Altschul, New York.

Below left

3-37. *Bo-Peep*, 1878. Gouache, 6⅞ x 8½ inches. Courtesy, Museum of Fine Arts, Boston. Bequest of John T. Spaulding.

Below right

3-38. *The Sick Chicken*, 1874. Watercolor, 9⅜ x 7⅜ inches. Colby College Art Museum, Waterville, Maine. The Harold T. Pulsifer Memorial Collection.

Opposite

3-39. *Morning Glories*, 1873. Watercolor, 19½ x 13¼ inches. Collection of Mr. and Mrs. John W. Warner.

Above

3-40. *The Carnival*, 1877. Oil on canvas, 20 x 30 inches. The Metropolitan Museum of Art. Lazarus Fund, 1922.

Left

3-41. *Shepherd and Shepherdess*, 1878. Twelve tiles, each 8 inches square. Collection of Mr. and Mrs. Arthur G. Altschul, New York.

Above
3-42. *The Two Guides*, 1876. Oil on canvas, 24 x 40 inches. Sterling and Francine Clark Art Institute, Williamstown, Massachusetts.

Right
3-43. *Watermelon Boys*, 1876. Oil on canvas, 24⅛ x 38⅛ inches. Cooper-Hewitt Museum of Decorative Arts and Design, Smithsonian Institution, New York.

Left
3-44. *The Green Dory*, 1880. Watercolor, 13½ x 19½ inches. Courtesy, Museum of Fine Arts, Boston. Bequest of Arthur Tracy Cabot.

Below
3-45. *Boy and Fallen Tree*, c. 1879. Watercolor, 8 x 11 inches. Courtesy, Museum of Fine Arts, Boston. Bequest of Estate of Katharine Dexter McCormick.

4

A Stern Poetry of Feeling

AN INTIMATION of the change in style and mood of Homer's painting that is catalyzed in the English trip appears in his work of 1880. *Promenade on the Beach* reflects his debt to French painting (ILL. 4–3 and COLOR PLATE 24), but it also possesses a new sobriety and somberness. Like Boudin and Monet in the 1860's, Homer favored the subjects of elegant ladies strolling along coastal beaches (although Homer continues to stress depth recession in a distinctively American manner). The change of feeling in this 1880 picture is evident when one compares it with *Long Branch, New Jersey* of just over a decade earlier (COLOR PLATE 12), a painting altogether lighter, gayer, and more animated. The sense of stillness in *Promenade on the Beach* is attributable to the starkly simplified design and the darker color scheme. Given Homer's gradual artistic maturation during the 1870's, one can feel his almost subconscious probing toward a new style. With full confidence in his technical mastery of both oil and watercolor, he had clearly reached a potentially critical point in his development. Homer probably recognized this in making his decision to leave for England during the spring of 1881. He needed to detach himself from the routine of the preceding years—to contemplate and work on his painting from a fresh vantage point. He found partial, but necessary, isolation near the Northumberland coastal town of Tynemouth.

He rented a small cottage in the neighboring fishing village of Cullercoats, situated where the mouth of the Tyne River opens out to the North Sea. It was a rugged coastline and life was not easy for those who had to fish in the face of frequently rough weather. Now for the first time in his art, Homer begins to show a real awareness of the natural and human drama of survival. His figures are more heroic, his subjects more serious, although he did produce several watercolors of local women quietly standing or walking in colorful gardens behind the stone walls of cottages like his own. Evidently he lived and worked alone, cooking for himself and generally remaining secluded.[1]

Homer worked hard during this period, concentrating almost exclusively on watercolor. His themes were largely those of storm and survival, shipwreck and rescue, fishermen at sea and their womenfolk waiting on shore. The possibility and the actuality of loss of life at sea were everpresent; the twin towns of North and South Shields at the mouth of the Tyne were known for their systems of rescue by lifeboat and the Volunteer Life Brigade.[2] Nature's forces were constantly testing human fortitude here, and in this milieu Homer found the new subject matter he seemed to be searching for. Characteristic is *Inside the Bar* (ILL. 4–1), a watercolor completed after his return to America. Instead of the bright colors and leisurely activities of his Gloucester watercolors (COLOR PLATES 15 and 23), there is now a pervasive grayness and monochromy. Figures are frequently seen isolated and alone, purposefully pursuing their tasks. They move with a slower step and a more sculptural stance. Nature's presence is fully evident in the brooding atmospheric effects and the stark emphasis on powerful rock ledges, strong winds, and dashing waves.

There are also technical changes in these Tynemouth watercolors. Homer was clearly working almost entirely out-of-doors, sketching directly from nature. A greater fluidity enters his handling of the washes, and within his consciously limited palette he achieves a forceful expressiveness. He matches the gravity of his subjects with an appropriate stillness of form and darkening of color. The loose, suggestive effects of his Tynemouth watercolors were partially in response to the climate and geography of the place. But they also may have derived from the watercolors of John Constable and J. M. W. Turner, among the most popular English painters of the nineteenth century. Turner especially had an influential champion in America and England in the critic John Ruskin. Homer had already been introduced to English sources during his early training at Bufford's; it would have been logical now to look at the best known of the English watercolorists firsthand. In addition, the Tynemouth-Shields area had long been a popular attraction for English artists. Earlier in the century, painters as diverse as Turner, Robert Salmon, and J. C. Ibbetson had worked along this area of the coast. There is little way of knowing if Homer knew their work, but the plein-air freshness and broad, loose washes of his work could well have resulted from exposure at this time to the English watercolorists.

Another, more probable source for the large, monumental fisherwomen who fill so many of these watercolors may have been Pre-Raphaelite painting, particularly that of Edward Burne-Jones. Also favorites of Ruskin, the Pre-Raphaelites had created a style that was widely popular in England in the middle decades of the century. Homer almost certainly knew something of their work from his days as an illustrator in Boston. Drawings by Burne-Jones, Edwin Landseer, John Everett Millais, and Dante Gabriel Rossetti were published in several art magazines during the 1860's and 70's, and their influence was strongly felt in the work of illustrators on both sides of the Atlantic.[3] Many of Homer's engravings for

Harper's and *Our Young Folks* reflect some familiarity with the English tradition. Besides knowing it from books and magazines, he could also have seen pictures firsthand in the English manner on exhibit in New York. Henry James, for example, commenting on the annual Water-Color Exhibition of 1875, which included some two dozen drawings and watercolors by Homer (described as "raw aquarelles"), noted that "the most interesting things, however, were not American. These consisted of some four elaborately finished pictures by Mrs. Spartali Stillman, who works in England under the shadow of Messrs. Burne-Jones and Rossetti."[4]

Burne-Jones's drawing *Seated Woman*, 1864 (ILL. 4–2), is characteristic of his Pre-Raphaelite manner. She sits almost immobile, covered in heavy, clinging drapery. Solidly modeled and simplified into large geometric volumes, she has an air of classical calm and timelessness. This very sense of physical presence and endurance was precisely the effect Homer sought for his own subjects, and aspects of Burne-Jones's style are evident in many of the Tynemouth watercolors of the early 1880's. Similar massive and monumental figures appear not only in *Inside the Bar* but also in other familiar works of this time, such as *Mending the Nets* (Collection Mr. and Mrs. Solton Engle), *Fisherfolk on the Beach at Tynemouth* (COLOR PLATE 25), *Looking Over the Cliff* (Plainfield Public Library, N.J.), *Hark! The Lark* (COLOR PLATE 26), an oil painted in 1882 and reworked in watercolor a year later as *A Voice from the Cliffs* (Collection Mrs. Charlotte Ford Niarchos). Absorbed and imperturbable, these women carry baskets of provisions or fishing nets—activities that draw attention to the hard life of the sea. These are not sensuous or even particularly feminine women; rather, they are statuesque figures of heroic endurance and self-reliance. Homer perceived in them and their lives both the physical power of nature and the solid resourcefulness of the human condition.

Still another possible influence on the formation of Homer's English style must be considered: the Elgin marbles in the British Museum. This major sculptural assemblage from the frieze and pediments of the Parthenon has comprised one of the world's great collections of antique art since they were brought from Greece in the first decade of the nineteenth century by Lord Elgin. For an artist who had been to the Louvre a decade earlier, had visited the Universal Exposition, and probably had seen other pictures by French painters, these famous pieces in England's greatest museum would surely have held some attraction. Homer must have had to pass through London on his way to and back from Tynemouth. He painted in the North Sea town during the summer seasons of 1881 and 1882. Although it is probable that he returned briefly to the United States for the intervening winter,[5] quite possibly he also spent some of it in London. In 1881, he painted at least one picture in the city, *The Houses of Parliament* (Collection Joseph Hirshhorn). Its concentration on the evanescent sparkle of light and water reflections recalls Turner's earlier versions of the subject, while also anticipating Monet's treatment of the same theme. At the Royal Academy in 1882, he exhibited several pictures, giving his address as Cullercoats.

But more convincing than speculation on Homer's physical movements during these months is the stylistic evidence in his work. The rounded classical heads, the massive, stately bodies, the wet, form-defining draperies—in fact, the whole air of heroic calm and timeless humanity—appear to have derived from the Parthenon marbles (ILL. 4–4). What better inspiration for Homer's sturdy, impersonal subjects? His biographers have remarked on the new *statuesque* and *sculptural* qualities of his figures, their greater roundness and solidity.[6] It is clear, too, that his subjects are no longer individualized, as they so frequently were in the preceding Gloucester watercolors (see ILL. 3–23), but generalized types engaged in common chores. Certainly the Parthenon sculptures could have influenced Homer's graver treatment of human beings both conceptually and technically. Alone, the Tynemouth climate and geography, the tight finish and large forms of Pre-Raphaelite painting, or the expressive fluidity of English watercolorists such as Turner do not fully explain Homer's new breadth of style and meaning at this time. Yet the accumulated experience of this year and a half in England did help him articulate a changed attitude toward his art.

Stalwart women were not Homer's only subjects in the early 1880's; he also painted the fishermen at Tynemouth, and later off the Maine coast and the Grand Banks, hauling their nets at sea. *The Herring Net* (COLOR PLATE 27) is a characteristic example from a series of the mid-1880's on this theme tried in different media. For example, he now began to use charcoal and white chalk for preliminary drawings. Unlike pen or pencil, these crayons permitted soft textural effects and a broad improvisory quality that well suited the mood of these works. Working with a neutral paper of gray or tan, and the charcoal or chalk, Homer could work with a wider range of dark and light tonalities. Closely related to this oil are the watercolor *Dory* and the charcoal drawing *A Haul of Herring* (ILLS. 4–5 and 4–6). In each, a pair of fishermen bend over their nets to haul in the catch. The figures and setting are anonymous; in one case, the men are alone at sea, in the other, schooners are visible on the horizon behind them. The preparatory charcoal drawing for *The Herring Net* (ILL. 4–7) shows the white sails of two vessels nearby the men at work in their dory. It is significant that in the final oil (COLOR PLATE 27) Homer increases the sense of isolation and universality by pushing these auxiliary vessels far off to the misty horizon.

A fuller understanding of the stylistic change in Homer's art may be obtained by comparing this oil with *Breezing Up* (COLOR PLATE 19), Homer's major marine of the preceding years. Both pictures show a boat seen on the diagonal. The silhouettes of figures fill the center of each composition. In the distance, another sailing vessel counterpoints the forms in the foreground. But beneath these surface similarities are substantial differences. In the earlier picture, bright coloring, the activity of the boat in motion (enhanced by the distant schooner), the formal liveliness of the silhouetted boys create an ambience of fun and excitement. Moreover, the faces of the participants are visible—their individual identities and their personal responses are evident. Even the spectator is drawn close by the open cockpit and the lines of sail leading his eye directly into the action. In contrast to all this, *The Herring Net* has a restrained and somber coloring. The boat sits balanced on the wave. The silhouettes of men and vessel are tightly drawn together in work related not to pleasure but to survival. Their faces are turned down and unseen; the anonymity complements the open, unidentifiable setting. Instead of youths enjoying a carefree sail close to the Gloucester shore, we are shown men methodically laboring far out on an impersonal sea. (Although the picture was painted in the mid-1880's after Homer returned to Maine, it is a subject he first found in Tynemouth and then developed in the years immediately following. This particular painting was in response to the arrival in 1884 of a great school of herring off the Maine coast. Homer rowed out with an acquaintance to make sketches of the fleet at work.)[7] Only a thin edge of the fishing net reaches the edge of the canvas, thus adding to the visual isolation of the figures. The stern of the dory is turned up to our eyes, one man's back faces us, both ignore us in their self-absorption.

Sometimes he undertook more dramatic and ambitious topics that included actual or implicit action and large numbers of figures. Such is the case with two 1881 watercolors, *Watching the Tempest* (ILL. 4–8) in which men ready lifeboats for launching when a let-up in the storm permits; and *Wreck of the "Iron Crown"* (Collection Mr. and Mrs. Carleton Mitchell), which was based on an event witnessed by the artist in October of that year. Men attempt to row a rescue boat out through the pounding surf to the stricken vessel on nearby rocks. Generally, these larger narratives are not as forceful as those pictures with single or few figures. Homer himself perhaps realized that they tended to be less expressive, belonging to the anecdotal and illustrational tradition of his earlier years, and such subjects held only infrequent interest for him in his later years. Gradually in his art he began to replace descriptions of narrative action with the concentrated drama of humanity struggling with nature's forces.

In November, 1882, he returned to the United States with a large group of watercolors, charcoal drawings, and some oils. The studies he had made abroad would provide source material for the next few years. Some pictures he finished in Maine, working up oils from Tynemouth sketches; others were obviously Maine subjects done in his new manner, with local figures occasionally looking transplanted from England to New England. At the Water Color Society in 1883, Homer exhibited four of his best English paintings, to the enthusiastic reception of the critics. As Mrs. Van Rensselaer wrote in the *Century:*

> "The Voice from the Cliffs" and "Inside the Bar" seem to me not only the most complete and beautiful things he has yet produced, but among the most interesting American art has yet created.... Homer does indeed, in these pictures, show something quite different from the fresh and individual but crude and unpoetic suggestiveness of his earlier aquarelles.... The dignity of these landscapes and the statuesque impressiveness and sturdy vigor of these figures, translated by the strong sincerity of his brush, prove an originality of mood, a vigor of conception, and a sort of stern poetry of feeling to which he had never reached before.[8]

Soon after his return from England, Homer decided to settle in Prout's Neck, Maine, where he was to live, except for occasional excursions, for the remainder of his life. Secluded at the end of a rocky point of land south of Portland, Prout's Neck was at that time no summer resort, but a small village populated mainly by farmers and fishermen. Like Cape Elizabeth just to the north, it projects out into the cold Atlantic. To many, it is the real beginning of the Maine coast, where rocks, evergreens, and water come together in strikingly beautiful combinations. This coast had held a special appeal for American artists since early in the century, when painters like Thomas Cole, Thomas Doughty, Alvan Fisher, Frederic Church, and Fitz Hugh Lane had come in search of pristine wilderness to paint. Homer was following in their footsteps when he, too, sought an understanding of man's relationship with the pure presence of nature.

Many of our now-familiar resort areas, such as Mount Desert, Maine; Narragansett Bay, Rhode Island; and Cape Ann, Massachusetts, first began to attract sizable numbers of visitors in the years after the Civil War. New possibilities for leisure life arose in the postwar period, due in part to advances in technology, which led to gradually reduced work weeks and to quicker modes of travel. Both artists and, soon after, vacationers made their way to these coastal areas that had the advantage of being at the same time accessible yet removed, civilized yet still raw in their beauty. The images American painters delineated of these places—for example, Cole and Church at Mount Desert; Whittredge, Heade, and Kensett at Newport; or Lane and Hassam at Cape Ann—often share the sense of reverence for nature's pristine expanses. Man's intruding presence is noted, but his immediate appearance is also seen as a part of a grander design and an unseen order. In Prout's Neck, Homer found such a place where he might realize and define his own sense of nature's meaning.

Homer's family had visited Prout's Neck during the 1870's, when he also came occasionally. His two brothers moved into houses of their own in 1882, and the next summer he occupied a converted studio on the top floor of Charles's house. Later he set up quarters in a nearby stable, outfitting his studio and building a porch that looked out over the cliffs and expanse of ocean. Evidently he felt comfortable and capable of productive work in this seclusion. The summer on Ten Pound Island at Gloucester in 1880 and the longer stay in Tynemouth during 1881–82 had given him time to consider himself and his art thoughtfully, to realize that such withdrawal was conducive for the creation of his best work.

His strongest pictures continued, for the most part, to be those of single individuals, usually struggling against the elements. Replacing the sculpturesque women of his Tynemouth period were the self-reliant fishermen of Maine. But the change from feminine to masculine subjects was less noticeable than the increasing emphasis on sheer physical endurance and human will. Here was a subject sufficiently profound that it became central to most of his later work. *The Fog Warning* (COLOR PLATE 28) was a natural evolution of the Tynemouth-inspired fishing scenes; it was one of a series of figures alone at sea that also included *Lost on the Grand Banks* (Collection John S. Broome) and culminated with *The Gulf Stream* (COLOR PLATE 44).

To paint his subject as realistically as possible, Homer persuaded one of his neighbors, Henry Lee, to pose in a dory that he had propped up on a sand dune at the beach. The dory was angled so as to suggest its rising on the crest of a wave, and for further accuracy the artist doused his sitter with a pail of water.[9] The situation of figure and boat again recalls *Breezing Up* of a decade earlier, but the isolation and monumentality of form present in *The Herring Net* mark these later works with a new starkness and force. In a composition that comes close but does not reach a monotonous symmetry, Homer deftly balances the crossing diagonals of the dory and wave crests. Other juxtapositions between the poised oars and horizon line, between the fisherman's glance and the threatening tongues of fog, and between the near and distant boats reinforce the sense of precarious safety here. Homer's brushwork is now much more vigorous than in any of his earlier oil painting. Just as his compositional arrangements are intended to suit the seriousness of his subjects, so, too, are the very texture and application of paint meant to reinforce the drama depicted on canvas.

The mid-1880's proved to be the beginning of an enormously productive period for Homer, who seems to have found his stride after returning from England. One of the major works of these years was *The Life Line*, 1884 (COLOR PLATE 29), which possesses a power and concentrated energy not quite attained in *The Fog Warning*. The theme was similar: human survival, only now presented in more immediate and dramatic terms. The composition was especially bold for Homer. Two figures are isolated against the flattened background of waves dashing on nearby rocks. They sit precariously swinging on the seat of the breeches buoy, with the shore on one side and the stricken vessel barely visible on the other. Much of the picture's intensity derives from the cropping of the outside elements at either side and from the curtain of water that presses toward the figures from behind. In this work, Homer has joined male and female together, heroically interlocking them with a complex tangle of limbs. In the initial pencil drawing (ILL. 4–9), he delineated the features of both figures carefully if generally, but the oil includes the important change of having the woman's scarf across her rescuer's face. This has the effect of intensifying the contrasts between life and lifelessness, action and inertia, ship and shore, man and nature. Both the flattened design and the device of cropping forms at the picture's edges are reminiscent of Japanese prints as well as of photographs, both of which Homer appears to have referred to occasionally throughout his later career.

The same year that he finished the oil, he also undertook to do an etched version (ILL. 4–10). About 1876, he had attempted his first etching, *Girl Posing in a Chair*, but now he took up the medium seriously, executing eight large plates between 1884 and 1889. The medium obviously suited Homer at this stage, since it allowed a relative freedom and ease of movement. To make an etching, one coats a metal plate with a resin or wax and draws in it with a pointed tool. After the image is drawn on the waxed plate, it is bathed in acid, permitting the plate to be eaten where not protected by the wax. Thus the acid does the hard work of biting the image into the metal, which is then inked and printed. The method itself, unlike the hardness of technique and effect in engraving, allowed Homer to reproduce the broad atmospheric qualities he was seeking to capture in his watercolors at the same time. Of the three printmaking techniques he took up in his life, this was probably the least successful for him, although for a time it did serve the large forms and fluid effects of his marine subjects. The etching of *The Life Line* crops his original design even further and eliminates more details, though in both he retains the foaming spume of water behind the figures, which sets off the tense pulley on the cable above. He reworked the composition yet another time in a second etching called *Saved*, done five years later. His other etchings included one done after a related subject, *Undertow* (see COLOR PLATE 30); three English subjects, *Mending Nets*, *Perils of the Sea* (see ILL. 4–15), and *A Voice from the Cliffs*; another marine, *Eight Bells* (see ILL. 4–11); and an Adirondack subject, *Fly Fishing, Saranac Lake*. In these, he made few compositional adjustments, sometimes changing a horizontal format, reversing the image, generalizing background details, or enlarging the figures. At the end of the 1880's, he gave up the medium, presumably because he could better achieve the fluent and atmospheric effects he wanted in watercolor. Also, the graphic medium essentially remained one of description and illustration, and this was a direction of decreasing interest after Tynemouth.

When the oil of *The Life Line* was exhibited at the National Academy in 1884, it was hailed by the critics as a masterpiece and was purchased at the then high price for Homer of $2,500.[10] It solidly bestowed on its author a major and indisputable reputation. Two years later, he essayed another oil of similar subject and design. *Undertow* (COLOR PLATE 30) shows four figures laterally extended across the picture, framed by a curling wave behind. With faces averted, the two men at either side have an anonymity similar to the purposeful fishermen painted a few years before. Between them are two interlocked figures close in arrangement to those in *The Life Line*. Again, Homer boldly sets off man and the force of the sea, just as once more he counterbalances men and women in the common experience of survival. The tight drawing of form, the solidly rounded figures, and the sense of almost sculptural immobility call to mind few other pictures in Homer's career. Among them would be *High Tide* and *Waiting for Dad* (COLOR PLATES 6 and 7). Here the seriousness of his theme dominates the picture, and part of the unusual stiffness may have been due to his renewed work in printmaking at this time. Nonetheless, he does manage to achieve a strong abstraction in the rhythmic forms of limbs and torsos. Some understanding of Homer's struggle with these forms may be sensed in the preliminary drawings for the two central figures (Clark Art Institute, Williamstown, Mass.). Intertwining them in various combinations, he also sought to play their shapes against the framing edges of his pages. Although he returned directly to a looser manner of composing and applying paint, the sense of pure form evident here continued to surface in subsequent paintings. He seemed to be testing yet another combination in his art of representation and abstraction, of the specific and the universal, the immediate and the timeless.

Large, dedicated, anonymous figures dominate the design of *Eight Bells* (ILL. 4–11), another important picture from 1886, this time based on the memory of experiences on his Atlantic crossing to Tynemouth. Although his neighbors Henry Lee and John Gatchell posed for the painting,[11] they become generalized in the ordinary operation on shipboard of shooting the sun with a sextant. But Homer raises the commonplace to a dignified, even heroic, level. By means of simplified design, concentration on major forms, and deemphasis of subordinate details, he strengthens the taut relationship of men and sea. The clouds are just parting—a storm has presumably just passed—and the men still dressed in oilskins are quietly making their observations. As he had done in his compositions of a decade before (compare COLOR PLATE 15 and ILL. 3–29), Homer echoes the two central figures with the pair of shrouds behind them and parallels the sextant, visually connecting the men with the thin ratlines to the right. In this way, he intimately links the animate and inanimate, the figural and the spatial. Equally important to the power of the final result is the expressive handling of paint and wide range of tonal contrasts. Together, Homer uses them all to create an image of disciplined thought and action. *Eight Bells* is both a moment in time and a condition of natural forces. The subsiding energy of the storm at sea is matched by the restrained concentration of the men at work, who plot their course at sea while metaphorically fixing their peace with nature.

With each new work, Homer was clarifying and deepening the meaning of his subjects. As he came to understand more profoundly the natural order and the human condition, he refined his technical means accordingly. The subtle changes he made from preliminary drawings, watercolors, or oil studies to the finished work demonstrated the process of distillation underlying the creative evolution of his imagery. This process is evident in most of the major late works but is nowhere more vivid than in the painting of *The Gale* (ILLS. 4–12 to 4–16 and COLOR PLATE 31). In 1881, he made a number of charcoal and pen sketches, as well as at least one watercolor, of various figures watching a storm on the boardwalk at Tynemouth. The dories are pulled up on the beach, and in one sketch fishermen are pointing out to sea, possibly discussing an imminent call for rescue. Now much more extensively exploiting the descriptive possibilities of different media, Homer tended to reserve pen and pencil for noting the gesture, posture, and action of figures, while employing charcoal or watercolor for effects of weather and atmosphere. Some sketches were devoted entirely to figural groupings, others to the more abstract arrangements of dories and building forms, and still others to the complex interrelationships between people, boats, and setting.

One watercolor in the 1881 group was sufficiently finished in itself to be given a title, *Perils of the Sea* (ILL. 4–15), and several years later Homer reversed the composition for one of his etchings. Now he has clarified the balance between the women on the boardwalk (no longer direct observers) and the men behind, directly concerned with the storm at sea. After he had returned to Maine, Homer reworked the subject in an even more simplified oil of 1883, *Coming Away of the Gale*, which is now known only from a surviv-

139

ing photograph (ILL. 4–16). Just the single figure moving against the wind, the one large dory, and the other clarified forms contain the essence of the storm. But the process of simplification was not the only factor at work here. Homer also made basic changes in composition by reversing the direction of the moving figure and placing her on a rocky ledge rather than the wooden boardwalk. These had the effect of heightening the confrontation of man and raw nature. While this was a stronger design than any of the earlier versions, Homer evidently was not fully satisfied, perhaps sensing, as we do, something hard and stiff in the arrangement of forms on the canvas. In any event, he put the picture aside for a decade.

When he came back to rework it in 1893 (COLOR PLATE 31), he transformed the English subject matter even further into a Maine setting by overpainting the Tynemouth watchtower and dory with the ledges of Prout's Neck. Over the grayish browns of his English palette, he also painted with much brighter and stronger greens, blues, and whites. Likewise, from the rather tight handling of pigment in the earlier version, he moved to a much fresher, bolder brushwork ten years later. Note especially the foaming waves as they dash upon the rocks. Homer had pushed his expressive power to yet a new level. As was characteristic of him, he uses a storm as the link between man and nature. The struggle is difficult but determined, as the powerful woman and child (still reminiscent of the Parthenon marbles) move forward with both bodily and spiritual will. This opposition of human and natural forces is at the heart of Homer's later paintings. The woman here moves resolutely forward across the massive rock ledge, facing the storm directly, and in other pictures of the nineties Homer further worked out this metaphor of individual struggle. For example, in *Winter Coast* and *The West Wind* (COLOR PLATES 39 and 41), he sets a solitary figure in a similarly desolate panorama of rugged cliffs and forceful storm. The vigor of Homer's color and brushwork in all of these images also enhances our sense of that raw, physical world he so reverently celebrated.

Homer submitted *The Gale* with fourteen others to the World's Columbian Exposition in Chicago in 1893 and was awarded the gold medal. Although other artists received similar awards, this was Homer's first public honor. Along with George Inness, he was one of the best represented painters at the exhibition. While there, he painted a small monochromatic oil (Bowdoin College, Brunswick, Maine) of Frederic Macmonnies's fountain in the central lagoon. In recording the electric lights at night, Homer saw in the fair one of the significant signs of a new age.

During the decade following his return from England, Homer also developed water-color as an expressive medium in its own right. Although he had executed watercolors during the previous decade at Gloucester and elsewhere, they were generally small and often peripheral to his principal artistic concerns. Often they served merely as initial studies of a subject, and only occasionally were they original statements in themselves. Tynemouth helped to alter that procedure. Working for a while almost entirely in watercolor, he developed a competence comparable to that already attained in oil. He moved steadily away from watercolor as a reportorial medium of basically drawing in color to one that took full advantage of the properties of wetness, quickness of execution, transparency, and spontaneity. Unlike the deliberations and corrections that were possible in oil, watercolor, Homer soon learned, should be enjoyed for its brightness and immediacy. In the watercolors of his mature career, the earlier concern for meticulously describing subject matter gradually yields to manipulating formal and technical aspects for their own dazzling effects. In the process of learning the distinctions of oil and watercolor, he slowly evolved relatively informal compositions for the latter medium. By the end of his career, he had produced a large number of sparkling, fresh watercolors, some of which are as bold and original as anything he did in oil.

Naturally, most of his themes in watercolor were similar to those he was working on in oil. He worked fairly consistently in both media side by side through the latter years of his life. However, on the whole, few of the watercolors approach the seriousness of subject or formality of design in the major oils. They tended to be more personal and intimate, usually recording the pleasures of a visit to the Caribbean or a fishing trip in the North woods. Yet their distinction makes his contribution in this medium comparable to that of Turner's in England.

Soon after settling in Prout's Neck, Homer began studies of the breakers along the cliffs in front of his studio. Typical of these watercolors were *Prout's Neck, Breakers* (Art Institute of Chicago), *The Northeaster* (Brooklyn Museum), both 1883, and *Breaking Wave* (ILL. 5–2) of 1887. Usually human beings were extraneous to these paintings—the drama of water, rocks, and light provided sufficient interest and challenge. Unlike the sense of mass and volume that preoccupied Homer in many of his oils, he was concerned here with action and movement. Less than the physical weight of water in collision with resisting rock masses, he sought to convey the fluidity, motion, and transparency of water. To this end, he allows the brilliant white of the paper to show through in several places, thus showing the action of light in and on the water. With such paintings, Homer tells us something about these waves entirely new and different from his oils.

Ordinarily Homer spent most of the year in Prout's Neck, with brief excursions in the fall to visit his brother Charles and his wife in West Townsend, Massachusetts, as well as the regular fishing trips during the spring or fall to Canada or the Adirondacks. To this routine he also added voyages, first, to the Bahamas in December, 1884, and again in 1885, and later to Florida in the winters of 1886, 1890, 1903, and 1904. From his first exposure to the southern sun, Homer was impressed with the intense sunlight and the brilliant colors of the landscape. His watercolors accordingly became filled with fresh, bright colors, which he handled with a sensibility that marked his style for the rest of his career. Recalling his pleasure in painting the dark skins and colorful costumes of the blacks he saw in Virginia during the mid-1870's, Homer was again attracted to the strong contrasts of color and texture he saw in the people, climate, and plant life of Nassau, Cuba, and Florida. He painted women going to market, street scenes, fishing boats, palm trees blown in the wind, and the intense blue waters of the coastline. In contrast to the cool and dark colors employed in his northern watercolors, here he stressed the vivid reds, blues, and yellows suitable for the intensely colored flowers and bright sunlight of the southern climate.

Homer continued to paint strong watercolors, mostly of Florida subjects (COLOR PLATE 38), through 1904. These included fishing boats off the Keys and fly-casting on rivers shaded by swaying palms. During the summer of 1906, he was ill for a long time, possibly from a minor stroke, and produced no work for several months. He still kept to himself in Prout's Neck, living entirely alone, happy to see his local neighbors but reluctant and often disagreeable with outside visitors. To his brother he wrote in 1895 that "the life that I have chosen gives me my full hours of enjoyment for the balance of my life."[12]

COLOR PLATE 23.
Children Playing Under a Gloucester Wharf, 1880. Watercolor, 8 x 13½ inches. Courtesy, Museum of Fine Arts, Boston. Hayden Collection.

143

COLOR PLATE 30.
Undertow, 1886. Oil on canvas, 30 x 47½ inches. Sterling and Francine Clark Art Institute, Williamstown, Massachusetts.

4-1. *Inside the Bar*, 1883. Watercolor, 15½ x 28½ inches. The Metropolitan Museum of Art. Gift of Louise Ryalls Arkell, 1954, in memory of her husband, Bartlett Arkell.

Left
Detail of Ill. 4-1.

Below
4-2. Edward Burne-Jones: *Seated Woman*, 1864. Charcoal on paper, 13 x 8½ inches. The Metropolitan Museum of Art. Gift of Harry G. Friedman, 1953.

152

4-3. Eugène Boudin: *Beach at Trouville*, 1863. Oil on panel, 7 x 13¾ inches. The Phillips Collection, Washington, D.C.

4-4. Phidias: *The Three Fates*, from the east pediment of the Parthenon, c. 438-431 B.C. The Trustees of the British Museum, London.

4-5. *The Dory*, c. 1884. Watercolor, 13¾ x 20¾ inches. Courtesy, Museum of Fine Arts, Boston. Hayden Collection.

4-6. *A Haul of Herring*, 1884. Charcoal and chalk on paper, 14⅞ x 23½ inches. Courtesy, Museum of Fine Arts, Boston. Bequest of George Nixon Black by exchange.

Opposite
4-7. Study for *The Herring Net*, 1885. Charcoal and chalk on paper, 16⅝ x 20⅝ inches. Cooper-Hewitt Museum of Decorative Arts and Design, Smithsonian Institution, New York.

Above
4-8. *Watching the Tempest*, 1881. Watercolor, 14 x 20 inches. Courtesy, Fogg Art Museum, Harvard University. Grenville L. Winthrop Bequest.

Above
4-9. Study for *The Life Line*, 1884. Charcoal and chalk on paper, 17½ x 11 inches. Cooper-Hewitt Museum of Decorative Arts and Design, Smithsonian Institution, New York.

Right
4-10. *The Life Line*, 1884. Etching, 12⅞ x 17¾ inches. The Metropolitan Museum of Art. Harris Brisbane Dick Fund, 1924.

4-11. *Eight Bells*, 1886. Oil on canvas, 25 x 30 inches. Addison Gallery of American Art, Phillips Academy, Andover, Massachusetts.

159

4-12. *Figures and Dories, Tynemouth Beach*, c. 1882. Pen and ink on paper, 7⅞ x 7⅛ inches. Cooper-Hewitt Museum of Decorative Arts and Design, Smithsonian Institution, New York.

4-13. *Beached Dories, Tynemouth*, c. 1882. Pen and ink on paper, 4¼ x 7⅛ inches. Cooper-Hewitt Museum of Decorative Arts and Design, Smithsonian Institution, New York.

4-14. *Two Women and a Child at a Rail, Overlooking Beach at Tynemouth*, c. 1882. Charcoal on paper, 8⅜ x 11¾ inches. Cooper-Hewitt Museum of Decorative Arts and Design, Smithsonian Institution, New York.

4-15. *Perils of the Sea*, 1881. Watercolor over charcoal on paper, 14⅝ x 21 inches. Sterling and Francine Clark Art Institute, Williamstown, Massachusetts.

4-16. *Coming Away of the Gale*, 1883. Photograph of the painting in its original state. Homer Collection, Bowdoin College Museum of Art, Brunswick, Maine.

COLOR PLATE 31.
The Gale, 1893. Oil on canvas, 30¼ x 48⅜ inches. Worcester Art Museum, Worcester, Massachusetts.

163

COLOR PLATE 32.

Northeaster, 1895. Oil on canvas, 34½ x 50 inches. The Metropolitan Museum of Art. Gift of George A. Hearn, 1910.

Below
COLOR PLATE 33.
Adirondack Guide, 1894. Watercolor, 15 x 21 inches. Courtesy, Museum of Fine Arts, Boston. Warren Collection.

Page 166
COLOR PLATE 34.
Old Friends, 1894. Watercolor, 21½ x 15⅛ inches. Worcester Art Museum, Worcester, Massachusetts.

themes of his oil paintings (such as *The Life Line, Eight Bells, Undertow*, etc.), they also celebrate physical exertion and the discipline of exercise. Similarly, Homer seldom includes more than a couple of figures, and they are always seen closely involved in the natural setting. Some do intimate a mood of seriousness similar to that in the major oils. For example, Homer often prefers to depict his fishermen or huntsmen from behind (ILL. 5–6), thus suggesting that sense of detachment from the viewer, that solitude first articulated in the Tynemouth period paintings (see COLOR PLATE 27). In *Canoe in the Rapids*, two men are paddling away from us into their own world of vigorous physical testing. Such pictures are paradoxically ones of both action and contemplation. In addition, Homer perfectly captures the cool light and climate of the North with predominantly green, blue, and pearly washes.

Many of these paintings also owe a strong debt to Homer's familiarity with photography, which, as we have seen, most likely extended back to his Civil War days (ILL. 2–8 and COLOR PLATE 4). Sometime after 1888, Charles Homer gave his brother an Eastman Kodak No. 1, a relatively small and advanced camera that could take over one hundred circular photographs on roll film.[2] Homer made use of this recently introduced model on several fishing trips to the Adirondacks and Florida during the next few years. Most of his photographs (ILL. 5–7) and those taken by his brother are of men paddling or casting from canoes, though a few are of camps in the woods. Clearly they provided the artist with a record of details, landscape panoramas, or light effects that might well provide ideas for subsequent pictures. By no means did he want to copy a painting from a photograph, but there is little question that the stopped action and stilled time of photography well suited subjects he was then painting. For example, there is a close relationship between these prints and the single canoe set off in the center distance of many Adirondack watercolors. More interesting is the apparent influence photography had on these pictures depicting trout leaping in the foreground, stopped and flattened on the surface of the painting.

Such is the case with *Trout Breaking* of 1889, *Ouananiche Fishing* of 1892, and *A Good Pool, Saguenay River*, 1895 (ILLS. 5–8 to 5–10). Evident is the photographic flattening of forms and of space—the horizon is obscured by the strong patterns made by water surface, spray, dark sky. In some of these watercolors, Homer takes a viewpoint looking down on the surface of the water, using its uniform darkness as a flat screen for the bright fish or its reflection in front. Particularly new and daring was his use of a vantage point looking back at the men from the position of the fish. Although naturally interested in the formal parallels between the shapes of the fish and the canoe, he is indebted to his photographs for the striking juxtaposition in a single frame of the different scale of men and fish, whose sizes are reversed because of the viewpoint. Such arbitrary illusions of scale and an imagery of stopped action were important new elements in his art at this time, and would continue to affect his painting up to the final and boldest works of his career, including the remarkable *Right and Left* of 1909 (COLOR PLATE 50).

Occasionally, touches of humor enter these watercolors, as in the playful contrast in *Trout Breaking* (ILL. 5–9) of the jumping fish and two butterflies hovering nearby. Both are caught in time by the artist's eye, two different speeds of movement and shapes in space. The beautiful *Mink Pond* of 1891 (COLOR PLATE 35) squares off in an amusing juxtaposition the frog and waterlily from their balanced positions on either side of the page. Still, these remain touching close-ups (again in a photographic sense) of the natural world that Homer so devotedly celebrated. In other instances, his intimate depictions of animal life touched upon the humanity of death. Flight and pursuit, survival and rescue, whether for man or animal, were much the same. In 1892, Homer painted a watercolor of a *Deer Drinking* (private collection); he chose almost the same format for a similar but far more poignant picture, *Fallen Deer* (ILL. 5–11). Meeting its death at the water's edge, the animal droops its head finally across the log into the limpid pool. Isolated, graceful, the deer is a haunting image of mortality. Man is not present (he would be an intrusion), although his hand is evident. Appropriately, Homer paints the subject in muted colors and darkened shadows.

By contrast, his southern watercolors are bright in color and warm in feeling. The sense of nature's profusion—the fullness of growth possible in such places—is apparent in paintings such as *Under the Coco Palm*, 1898 (ILL. 5–12). The twin shapes of the coconut and the boys' head are at the center of an effusion of colorful flowers and leaves. Characteristically, it is a painting of felt warmth and implied well-being.

One of Homer's finest southern watercolors was his *Sloop, Nassau* of 1899 (COLOR PLATE 37) with its vivid concentration of form and coloring, strong simplicity of design, and utter control of medium. Equally striking were two similar subjects of the same period, *The Turtle Pound* (COLOR PLATE 36) and *Stowing Sail, Bahamas* (ILL. 5–15). In all of them, Homer plays off the principal elements of dark-skinned fishermen, white sails, and green-blue water. Sometimes he seemed mainly interested in the abstract rhythms of repeated sails or masts and hulls. In *Sloop, Nassau* the furled sails and their bright reflections in the water create the central focus of his design. The curving furls possess an abstract rhythm that is fixed against the dark blue sky behind them. By working from the bare white paper in the center to the dark washes at the side, Homer establishes a vivid range of tonal contrasts. His brushwork is free and sure, the strokes of wash broad, swift, and expressive. It is remarkable that he should so readily achieve an effect at once of ease and drama.

Some measure of his achievement may be understood by comparing this work to one of John Singer Sargent's watercolors. Although very much American by genealogy, Sargent grew up and spent much of his time abroad in the fashionable circles of Europe. He cultivated an easy technical ability in both oil and watercolor. With complete confidence and dexterity he could produce a dazzling portrait or landscape. Yet alongside Homer's watercolors, Sargent's watercolors seem lacking in structure, concentration, or economy. For example, *White Ships* (ILL. 5–14) is filled with diverting details and no focus of attention.

Shooting the Rapids, Saguenay River (ILL. 5–28) of 1905 remained unfinished. Based on a watercolor done three years earlier, the oil retains Homer's characteristic vigor and energy. His brother Charles clings to the center of the canoe while the guides paddle intensely through the churning water. Man's struggle with the elements is still a personal one for Homer, though the uncompleted canvas gave poignant testimony to the artist's failing reserves. During the summer of 1908, Homer suffered a partially paralytic stroke. In the last few years, he had not been able to sustain his former rate of production, and occasionally he even determined in frustration to give up painting altogether. But by the fall of that year, his creative urges had risen again. At Thanksgiving he purchased two wild ducks, but the color of their plumage so appealed to him that he began to paint instead of eat them. The result was *Right and Left* in which the ducks are shown in flat rhythmic patterns on the picture surface. Barely visible in the left distance are hunters in a boat; one has just fired his double-barrel shotgun to bring down the birds with successive shots (hence the title). The viewpoint is so low that any horizon is obscured almost fully. The spectator looks back from the vantage of the birds toward the hunters in the distance. Seen in stopped photographic action, one rises and one falls—that favorite device of pairing opposites. Putting the viewer with the birds has the effect of vaguely disturbing our own sense of humanity. By painting the ducks caught in the very moment between life and death, he holds in suspension forever the meaning of mortality.

After this, he completed only one more painting, *Driftwood* (ILL. 5–30). The active brushwork for a final time brings into harmonious union man in solitude with the sea. An old log has drifted ashore, bringing its impersonal history from the deep. The coastline as metaphor for the edge of the unknown was the fitting terminus for Homer's old age. He suffered from digestive trouble and stomach pain. His health continued to fail through the summer of 1910, until blindness struck from internal hemorrhaging. Earlier he had protested to his family that "all is lovely outside my house & inside of my house & myself."[13] With his brothers nearby, he died of heart failure on September 29.

Winslow Homer was a special artist in not letting time pass him by. Though he was affected by the artistic currents of his century, he never imitated or borrowed directly. His stature as a painter increased to the end of his life. Looking again at his pictures makes one realize that what Robert Frost called "inner and outer weather" was for Homer the same thing.

179

Page 179
COLOR PLATE 35.
The Mink Pond, 1891. Watercolor, 13⅞ x 20 inches. Courtesy, Fogg Art Museum, Harvard University. Grenville L. Winthrop Bequest.

COLOR PLATE 36.
The Turtle Pound, 1898. Watercolor, 14 15/16 x 21⅜ inches. The Brooklyn Museum. A. T. White Memorial Fund and Others.

COLOR PLATE 37.
Sloop, Nassau, 1899. Watercolor, 15 x 21½ inches. The Metropolitan Museum of Art. Amelia B. Lazarus Fund, 1910.

COLOR PLATE 42.
The Fox Hunt, 1893. Oil on canvas, 38 x 68 inches. Courtesy, Pennsylvania Academy of the Fine Arts, Philadelphia.

5-1. *Cannon Rock*, 1895. Oil on canvas, 38⅛ x 29⅛ inches. The Metropolitan Museum of Art. Gift of George A. Hearn, 1906.

Left

5-2. *Breaking Wave*, 1887. Watercolor, 14 x 20¼ inches. Courtesy, Museum of Fine Arts, Boston. Bigelow Collection.

Below

5-3. *Coast in Winter*, 1892. Oil on canvas, 28⅜ x 48⅜ inches. Worcester Art Museum. Theodore T. and Mary G. Ellis collection.

188

5-4. *Clamming*, 1887. Watercolor, 10⅞ x 20⅛ inches. Courtesy, Museum of Fine Arts, Boston. Gift of John S. Ames.

5-5. *Hillside with Trees*, 1895. Watercolor, gouache, and pencil on paper, 3 x 20 inches. Cooper-Hewitt Museum of Decorative Arts and Design, Smithsonian Institution, New York.

Below

5-6. *Canoe in the Rapids*, 1897. Watercolor, 13½ x 20½ inches. Courtesy, Fogg Art Museum, Harvard University. Louise E. Bettens Fund.

Opposite

5-7. *Canoeist, Lake St. John, Province of Quebec*, c. 1895. Photograph, diameter 2⅝ inches. Homer Collection, Bowdoin College Museum of Art, Brunswick, Maine.

191

Opposite and right

5-8. *Ouananiche Fishing, Lake St. George, Quebec*, 1892. Watercolor, 14 x 20¾ inches. Courtesy, Museum of Fine Arts, Boston. Warren Collection.

Center

5-9. *Trout Breaking*, 1889. Watercolor, 13⅝ x 19⅝ inches. Courtesy, Museum of Fine Arts, Boston. Bequest of John T. Spaulding.

Below

5-10. *A Good Pool, Saguenay River*, 1895. Watercolor over pencil on paper, 9¾ x 18⅞ inches. Sterling and Francine Clark Art Institute, Williamstown, Massachusetts.

193

5-11. *Fallen Deer*, 1902. Watercolor, 13¾ x 19¾ inches. Courtesy, Museum of Fine Arts, Boston. Hayden Collection.

5-12. *Under the Coco Palm*, 1898. Watercolor, 14⅜ x 20½ inches. Courtesy, Fogg Art Museum, Harvard University. Louise E. Bettens Fund.

Above

5-13. *Nassau*, 1899. Watercolor, 15 x 21 inches. The Metropolitan Museum of Art. Purchase: Amelia B. Lazarus Fund, 1910.

Left

5-14. John Singer Sargent: *White Ships*, 1908. Watercolor, 13⅝ x 19⅛ inches. Courtesy, The Brooklyn Museum.

5-15. *Stowing Sail, Bahamas*, 1903. Watercolor, 14 x 22 inches. The Art Institute of Chicago. Mr. and Mrs. Martin A. Ryerson Collection.

5-16. Hokusai: *Shower Before the Mountain*, c. 1830. Wood engraving, 9¾ x 14¾ inches.
The Metropolitan Museum of Art. The Howard Mansfield Collection, Rogers Fund, 1936.

COLOR PLATE 43.
The Artist's Studio in an Afternoon Fog, 1894. Oil on canvas, 24 x 30 inches. Memorial Art Gallery of the University of Rochester, New York. R. T. Miller Fund.

199

COLOR PLATE 44.
The Gulf Stream, 1899. Oil on canvas, 28 x 49 inches. The Metropolitan Museum of Art. Wolfe Fund.

COLOR PLATE 45.
After the Hurricane, Bahamas, 1899. Watercolor, 14⅜ x 21⅜ inches. The Art Institute of Chicago.
Mr. and Mrs. Martin A. Ryerson Collection.

Opposite
COLOR PLATE 46.
On a Lee Shore, 1900. Oil on canvas, 39 x 39 inches. Museum of Art, Rhode Island School of Design, Providence.

Above
COLOR PLATE 47.
West Point, Prout's Neck, 1900. Oil on canvas, 30¼ x 48¼ inches. Sterling and Francine Clark Art Institute, Williamstown, Massachusetts.

203

COLOR PLATE 48.
Eastern Point, Prout's Neck, 1900. Oil on canvas, 30 x 40 inches. Sterling and Francine Clark Art Institute, Williamstown, Massachusetts.

Kissing the Moon, 1904. Oil on canvas, 30 x 40 inches. Addison Gallery of American Art, Phillips Academy, Andover, Massachusetts.

COLOR PLATE 50.
Right and Left, 1909. Oil on canvas, 28¼ x 48 inches. National Gallery of Art, Washington, D.C. Gift of Avalon Foundation.

Above
5-17. *A Moonlit Sea*, 1890. Watercolor, 14½ x 21½ inches. Courtesy, Wadsworth Atheneum, Hartford, Connecticut. J. J. Goodwin Fund.

Right
5-18. *A Summer Night*, 1890. Oil on canvas, 20½ x 39¾ inches. Musée National d'Art Moderne, Paris.

Opposite
5-19. *The Lookout—"All's Well,"* 1896. Oil on canvas, 40 x 30¼ inches. Courtesy, Museum of Fine Arts, Boston. William Wilkins Warren Fund.

Above
5-20. Study for *The Lookout—"All's Well,"* 1896. Crayon and gouache on paper, 12½ x 13⅞ inches. Cooper-Hewitt Museum of Decorative Arts and Design, Smithsonian Institution, New York.

5-21. Studies for *The Lookout—"All's Well"* and *The Wreck*, 1896. Charcoal and gouache on paper, 10⅜ x 13¾ inches. Cooper-Hewitt Museum of Decorative Arts and Design, Smithsonian Institution, New York.

5-22. *The Wreck*, 1896. Oil on canvas, 30¼ x 48⅜ inches. Museum of Art, Carnegie Institute, Pittsburgh, Pennsylvania.

5-23. *The Gulf Stream*, 1899. Watercolor, 11 x 19½ inches. The Art Institute of Chicago. Mr. and Mrs. Martin A. Ryerson Collection.

5-24. Study for *West Point, Prout's Neck*, 1900.   Charcoal and chalk on paper, 12½ x 21⅝ inches. Cooper-Hewitt Museum of Decorative Arts and Design, Smithsonian Institution, New York.

Cannon by Winslow Homer
at Morro Castle Santiago de Cuba —

Opposite above

5-25. *The Old Guns at Morro Castle, Santiago de Cuba*, c. 1885. Pencil on paper, 4⅞ x 7⅞ inches. Cooper-Hewitt Museum of Decorative Arts and Design, Smithsonian Institution, New York.

Opposite below

5-26. *The Old Guns at Morro Castle, Santiago de Cuba*, c. 1885. Pencil and chalk on paper, 11 x 18⅝ inches. Cooper-Hewitt Museum of Decorative Arts and Design, Smithsonian Institution, New York.

Above

5-27. *Searchlight, Harbor Entrance, Santiago de Cuba*, 1901. Oil on canvas, 30⅝ x 50½ inches. The Metropolitan Museum of Art. Gift of George A. Hearn, 1906.

Opposite

5-28. *Shooting the Rapids, Saguenay River*, 1905. Oil over chalk on canvas, 30 x 48¼ inches. The Metropolitan Museum of Art. Gift of Charles S. Homer, 1911.

Below

5-29. Hokusai: *The Great Wave off Kanagawa*, c. 1830. Wood engraving, 10 x 15 inches. The Metropolitan Museum of Art. The Howard Mansfield Collection, Rogers Fund, 1936.

8. *Ibid.*, 238.

9. *Ibid.*, 288.

10. *Ibid.*, 217, 275–76.

11. John I. H. Baur, *Eastman Johnson* (exhibition catalogue, Brooklyn, 1940), 5.

12. *Ibid.*, 18–19.

13. *Ibid.*, 22; Goodrich, 37; and Patricia Hills, *Eastman Johnson* (New York, 1972), 79–82.

14. See Barbara Novak's discussion of this in *American Painting of the Nineteenth Century* (New York, 1969), 167–74.

15. Quoted in Goodrich, 39.

16. Gardner, 90.

17. William Howe Downes, quoted in Gardner, 89. Goodrich more or less agrees: "The influence of this trip on his art was not great," *op. cit.*, 40.

18. Gardner, 89.

19. Goodrich, 40.

20. Newhall, 30, 37, 40–41, 44.

21. Goodrich, 38. Also see discussions in Gardner, 93–118; and Novak, 166–67.

CHAPTER 3

1. Quoted in Goodrich, 51.

2. Goodrich, 56–57.

3. *Ibid.*, 24.

4. See John Wilmerding, "Interpretations of Place: Views of Gloucester, Mass., by American Artists," Essex Institute *Historical Collections* CIII (January, 1967), 53–65.

5. See Helen M. Knowlton, *The Art Life of William Morris Hunt* (Boston, 1900), 119.

6. Quoted in Goodrich, 70.

7. *Ibid.*, 168.

8. *Ibid.*, 60

9. "The Tile Club at Work," *Scribner's Monthly* XVII, no. 3 (January, 1879), 401–9.

10. See Mahonri Sharp Young, "The Tile Club Revisited," *The American Art Journal* II, no. 2 (Fall, 1970), 81–91.

11. Quoted in Goodrich, 61.

12. *Ibid.*, 53–54.

CHAPTER 4

1. Goodrich, 76.

2. *Ibid.*

3. Gardner, 156.

4. *Ibid.*, 194.

5. Goodrich, 76.

6. *Ibid.*, 77–79.

7. Philip C. Beam, *Winslow Homer at Prout's Neck* (Boston, 1966), 66–68.

8. Quoted in Goodrich, 80.

9. *Ibid.*, 91–92; and Beam, 69–71.

10. Goodrich, 87.

11. Beam, 81–82.

12. Goodrich, 114.

CHAPTER 5

1. Goodrich, 114.

2. Beam, 74–75.

3. Quoted in Beam, 95.

4. Quoted in Goodrich, 121.

5. Goodrich, 132–33; and Beam, 109–10.

6. Beam, 110.

7. Quoted in Goodrich, 140.

8. John W. Beatty, "Recollections," quoted in Goodrich, 218–19.

9. See Joel Porte, *The Romance in America* (Middletown, Conn., 1969), 152.

10. Quoted in Goodrich, 162.

11. *Ibid.*, 188.

12. *Ibid.*, 165.

13. *Ibid.*, 198.

Bibliography

Baur, John I. H. *Eastman Johnson, An American Genre Painter* (catalogue). Brooklyn, New York, 1940.

Beam, Philip C. *Winslow Homer at Prout's Neck*. Boston, 1966.

Cox, James M. *Mark Twain, The Fate of Humor*. Princeton, N.J., 1966.

Cox, Kenyon. *Winslow Homer*. New York, 1914.

Downes, William Howe. *The Life and Works of Winslow Homer*. Boston and New York, 1911.

Flexner, James Thomas. *The World of Winslow Homer*. New York, 1966.

Gardner, Albert Ten Eyck. *Winslow Homer, American Artist: His World and His Work*. New York, 1961.

Goodrich, Lloyd. *American Watercolor and Winslow Homer*. Minneapolis, 1945.

———. *The Graphic Art of Winslow Homer*. New York, 1968.

———. *Winslow Homer*. New York, 1944.

———. *Winslow Homer*. New York, 1959.

Hills, Patricia. *Eastman Johnson*. New York, 1972.

Hoopes, Donelson F. *Sargent Watercolors*. New York, 1970.

———. *Winslow Homer Watercolors*. New York, 1969.

Horan, James D. *Mathew Brady: Historian with a Camera*. New York, 1955.

———. *Timothy O'Sullivan: America's Forgotten Photographer*. New York, 1966.

Katz, Joseph, ed. *The Portable Stephen Crane*. New York, 1969.

Matthiessen, F. O. *American Renaissance: Art and Expression in the Age of Emerson and Whitman*. London, Toronto, and New York, 1941.

Melville, Herman. *Moby Dick*. New York: Modern Library, 1950.

Newhall, Beaumont. *The History of Photography from 1839 to the Present Day*. Rev. ed. New York, 1964.

Novak, Barbara. *American Painting of the Nineteenth Century*. New York, 1969.

PORTE, JOEL. *The Romance in America, Studies in Cooper, Poe, Hawthorne, Melville, and James*. Middletown, Conn., 1969.

WHITMAN, WALT. *Leaves of Grass*. New York: New American Library, 1954.

———. *Specimen Days*. Boston, 1971.

WILLIAMS, HERMANN WARNER, JR. *The Civil War: The Artists' Record* (catalogue). Washington, D.C., and Boston, 1961.

WILMERDING, JOHN. "Winslow Homer's Drawings," *Winslow Homer* (catalogue). New York, 1972.

YOUNG, MAHONRI SHARP. "The Tile Club Revisited." *The American Art Journal* II, no. 2 (Fall, 1970): 81–91.

Index

Design by Joseph Bourke Del Valle

Color plates printed by Henry Stone & Son, Banbury, England. Black and white plates printed by Halliday Lithograph Corp., U.S.A. Binding by Montauk Book Mfg. Co.